SUPERYOU

Hi Jason
welcome
home!

hope you enjoy
this.

All my love
Lorr /x x

By the same author:

Superlife
Superlove

SUPERYOU

Be the Best You Can Become

Anne Naylor

Thorsons
An Imprint of HarperCollinsPublishers

Thorsons
An Imprint of HarperCollins*Publishers*
77–85 Fulham Palace Road
Hammersmith, London W6 8JB

1160 Battery Street
San Francisco, California 94111–1213

Published by Thorsons 1996

1 3 5 7 9 10 8 6 4 2

A catalogue record for this book
is available from the British Library

ISBN 0 7225 3146 X

Printed in Great Britain by
HarperCollinsManufacturing Glasgow

To SuperYou, the reader,
and *your* **Possible Dream**.

With God, all things are possible.
So, what do you want?
John Morton

Our deepest fear is not that we are inadequate. Our deepest fear is that we are powerful beyond measure. It is our light, not our darkness, that most frightens us. We ask ourselves, who am I to be brilliant, gorgeous, talented and fabulous? You are a child of God. Your playing small doesn't serve the world. We are born to make manifest the glory of God within us. It's not just in some of us, it's in everyone. And as we let our own light shine , we unconsciously give other people permission to do the same. As we are liberated from our own fear, our presence automatically liberates others.

Nelson Mandela
Inaugural Speech, 1994

Contents

Index of Exercises

INDEX OF EXERCISES

Acknowledgements

SuperYou has been written from my heart and has been an adventure of learning to practise living with a positive focus, to meet and overcome my own fears and resistance to necessary change; learning to surrender the control over life I thought I needed to live a fulfilling and rewarding life; learning how enriching life becomes as I wake up to the abundance of possibilities available to me to expand into it, to give and receive in greater ways.

My deep gratitude goes to John Roger and John Morton, whose work is a constant source of inspiration and encouragement to me and has assisted me more than I can ever put into words to reveal the SuperYou in me and the capacity I have to realize my **Possible Dream**.

In the production of *SuperYou*, the book, my thanks go to Jane Graham-Maw at Thorsons for her support and to Lizzie Hutchins for her patient editing of my manuscript. I am also deeply grateful to Gina Sussens — her capacity for caring and truly listening has been a tremendous support as I have been living through the production of *SuperYou*.

My thanks also go to dear friends – in the Santa Barbara, California, area, especially to Marian Bateman, Teresa Healey, Andra Carasso and Betsy Taylor; in London, to Nathalie Franks; in France, to Lois and Dushyant Patel, whose Thursday evenings in Vence have opened doors to many wonderful new friends and opportunities to share

ACKNOWLEDGEMENTS

my work. I have especially appreciated the encouragement I have received from Nikki Williams and our 'Problem Aired' chats on Monte Carlo's Riviera Radio.

None of my writing would be possible without the solid foundation of my caring family, Mum and Dad, Diana and David, who give me the background to explore new ways of living more courageously.

My heartfelt gratitude also goes to Paddy Naylor — your loving kindness and the inspiration of your life's work have shown me how extraordinary, and as yet untapped, is the immense wealth of human energy and resource in the world. Your creative genius for transforming what seem to be impossibly difficult predicaments into brilliantly possible solutions has encouraged me to know that I *can* realize the **Possible Dream** in my heart.

Introduction

SuperYou: Be the best you can become is a manual for self-management offering a strategy for achieving your **Possible Dream**. What is your **Possible Dream**? It is your optimal health and well-being; personal empowerment and compassion in your relationships; and clarity of purpose and direction in your occupation or vocational pursuits. It becomes a way of being, of living from the heart, motivated by a keen sense of purpose that is defined by your personal values, meaning and connectedness with the world around you. It might be best viewed as an adventure of exploration and discovery, carried out moment by moment.

By knowing clearly what you want in your heart of hearts and gaining personal direction over your life, you will be able to overcome any self-imposed limiting beliefs, conditions, unhealthy dependencies and addictions you may face. *SuperYou* will show you how to practise the self-care required to negotiate your way effectively around the uncertainties and difficulties of this increasingly changing world.

In work and finances, family and personal relationships, traditional views and values are at a turning-point. The greatest challenge we face at turning-points in life is that of fear: fear of losing control of our lives, fear of being abandoned by the ones we love, fear of the unknown, fear that we might not be able to attain what it is we most want. Seen positively, however, fear can be an asset. In *SuperYou*, you will discover how to reconnect yourself with your wealth of inner resources. You will be able to gain the altitude and attitude to perceive changes as tremendous opportunities for personal expansion, growth and outstanding accomplishment.

Working the SuperYou Trilogy

Superyou completes the trilogy of *Superlife: The seven steps that spell SUCCESS* and *Superlove: The guide to happiness in personal relationships* by helping you to recognize your intrinsic value, nurturing your sense of esteem and developing the necessary confidence to make the most of your life.

SUPERLIFE (3)
Typically, we are educated to place most of our life eggs in the material/career/financial basket. In this area, we are vulnerable to external changes (such as global economic movements) over which we as individuals, including the experts, have absolutely no control. To make this area our main, or only, focus is very disempowering.

SUPERLOVE (2)
We have marginally more control in this area – but have you ever tried to change your nearest and dearest? Your child, parent, mother-in-law – or even your boss, employee or work colleague? You *may* have choice in those with whom you spend time. You *do* have choice in *how* you relate with other people, especially in the attitudes you adopt towards them.

SUPERYOU (1)

It is in the personal area that we have the greatest potential choice and control. Our success and fulfilment in the other two areas hang from the strength and power of our intention in this area.

Innergetics©

By learning how to create a clear intention and maintain a positive focus, you will discover how you, as SuperYou, can realize your **Possible Dream**, from the inside out. The symbol **(I)** is used to draw your attention to your inner worlds of thinking, feeling and imagination, in which you can exercise greatest freedom of choice. **(O)** is used to refer to the outer world of other people, events and circumstances, which is usually beyond your direct control. The relationship between **(I)** and **(O)** is described as **Innergetics©**.

Innergetics©, the art and science of positive focusing, will provide you with the methods and techniques with which you can daily exercise higher levels of choice and creativity. By appreciating your inherent worth and by honouring your personal values and inner motivations, you will be enabled to achieve the results you seek. As you become committed to fulfilling your own aspirations in all areas of your life, you will experience much greater enthusiasm, initiative, freedom, pleasure and enjoyment.

SuperYou offers you a practical way forward to take charge of your life, with simple exercises and clear examples. Whether you are a banker or a housewife, a teacher or a student, a politician or a doctor, an opera singer or a market trader, a princess or a policeman, a bishop or a bookmaker, you are free to choose how you *experience* your life. You can drift aimlessly in a sea of doubt, resignation and indifference. Alternatively, you can choose to rise above the murky depths and ride the waves of extraordinary opportunity that are increasingly available for those who define their vision, their **Possible Dream**.

Be the best you can become – SuperYou will show you how.

1

Seeing the Dream

Recognizing Possibility

You see things that never were; and you say 'Why?'
But I dream things that never were; and I say 'Why
not?'
A miracle is an impossible thing that is nevertheless
possible. Something that could never happen, and yet
does happen.

George Bernard Shaw, *Back to Methuselah*

You may be all too familiar with the expression 'impossible
dream', both as a saying and from your own experience. So
what is the difference between a dream that is impossible
and the one that is possible? Consider the following:

- We live in a miraculous world, surrounded by the
  wonder of new life continually being born, human
  achievements that defy reason, beauty and intelligence
  in many forms.
- Each of us is abundantly endowed with *human energy
  and resource*, sufficient not only to sustain life at a basic
  level but also to derive extraordinary fulfilment,

1

happiness, joy and pleasure as an everyday reality.

- It takes *only one person* with a clearly defined vision and the willingness to make it happen to make an 'impossible' dream possible and effect seeming miracles.
- We are all *winners* in our lives – whatever we 'win' is what we have chosen to focus upon.
- We live in a world of *peace and plenty* where we can enjoy peace in the family and plenty in our purse. ('Family' refers here to any other member of the human race.)

Waking Up to Who You Are

Deep down, we all know what we most want to be, do and have in our lives. What if each of us is born with latent gifts for the purpose of enriching ourselves and others? It's not such a strange idea. Imagine your life as an adventure in which the beauty of your gifts is revealed to you, sometimes in surprising ways or through challenging circumstances. Those times which were difficult for you in the past could in hindsight be viewed as 'blessings in disguise' because you had to draw upon previously hidden reserves of personal strength.

Given that sooner or later most of us will encounter obstacles or challenges in some form, we have a choice. Either we may opt to 'let life happen to us', as a potential victim of whatever gets served up on our plate, or we can consciously take charge of our lives, knowingly meeting our challenges with courage and confidence. At any stage of our lives, having a purpose and setting a direction for ourselves is definitely the more rewarding choice.

The exercise that follows is a first step towards discovering your **Possible Dream**. It can be done right away, even if you later wish to review and revise your responses.

2

Revealing your **Dream** may be rather like peeling layers of an onion until you come to the centre of your life's purpose and fulfilment.

What Is *your* Possible Dream?

Questionnaire

The following brief questionnaire will assist you to begin clarifying your **Dream**. Do not be concerned if you have few answers to the questions immediately, or if they seem sketchy or incomplete. Those that are relevant for you will be answered, one way or another, in good time. Allow yourself to relax and enjoy the process.

1. Do you know your Possible Dream? Can you describe it in one sentence?
2. If you could make a single significant contribution to the world, what would that be?
3. What might stand in the way of you making that contribution:
    a. within yourself?
    b. from outside yourself?
4. Which of your personal strengths will most support you in making this contribution?
5. What skills do you need to develop?
6. What apparent limitations do you need to transform into assets in order to successfully fulfil your **Possible Dream**?
7. What are your first steps?

The answers to your questions might look something like this example:

1. Do you know your **Possible Dream**? Can you describe it in one sentence?
   I have no clear and comprehensive answer right now – but I shall do the exercise to see what I can find out. Meantime, I am going to say this affirmation every day:

   I know my **Possible Dream**.

2. If you could make a single significant contribution to the world, what would that be?
   Writing a book that makes a very constructive difference to a lot of people's lives. But I think there may be more to it than this.
3. What might stand in the way of you making that contribution:
   a. within yourself?
      A fear of criticism, personal rejection and, on the other hand, the results of being successful.
   b. from outside yourself?
      Nothing really, once I recognize that any obstacle that I perceive can be viewed as an asset.
4. Which of your personal strengths will most support you in making this contribution?
   Discipline, a sense of humour, determination, latent talent.
5. What skills do you need to develop?
   Patience with other people (and myself), improved communication skills generally (writing, speaking,

etc.), doing book promotions on radio and TV and anywhere else that might work well.

6. What apparent limitations do you need to transform into assets in order to successfully fulfil your **Possible Dream**?

Unspecified doubts as to whether I am capable of achieving what I really want. I am not sure how that could be turned into an 'asset' right now. My main limitations are really limiting beliefs that what I have to say is not really worthwhile, that no one would want to read it anyway, that it is all too difficult to achieve.

7. What are your first steps?

Eeek – this sounds like a commitment. I am not sure I like that.

Well, OK. Write the next page.

Taking Personal Responsibility – 100 Per Cent

There is a direct relationship between the results, events and people that show up in your life **(O)** and the inner reality **(I)** you hold about the way you are and the way life is. For example, you will have a hard job creating wealth in your life if you feel yourself to be unworthy of receiving it and believe that the world is lacking in the resources you need. Similarly, but more positively, when you love and support yourself by taking care of your physical, mental and emotional health and fitness, you will attract loving relationships in which you feel loved and supported. Like attracts like.

Is what you are thinking and doing in your life giving

you the results that you want? If not, it is within your power to change your perceptions, thoughts, beliefs and actions in order to create a more agreeable life for yourself. It has been said that:

The thoughts you hold produce states of consciousness;

States of consciousness persisted in produce physical outcomes.

With awareness, we can consciously exercise choice over the thoughts we hold. The good news is that we are responsible for everything that shows up in our lives, whether we initially interpret it as good or bad. Ultimately, everything can be of value to us. Taking responsibility in this way is a choice for personal empowerment, the ability we have to create more of what we do want and less of what we do not want. Responsibility is not the same as fault or blame. It is about accountability.

When we accept that we are 100 per cent responsible for whatever shows up in our lives, we may then say:

I can achieve my **Possible Dream**.

No matter what circumstances we encounter, we do have the *response-ability*, or *ability to respond*, with a positive choice **(I)** for upliftment. There is another aspect of taking responsibility which comes with the agreements we choose to make with ourselves and others. For example, we make an agreement with ourselves when we commit to a diet or exercise programme. When we choose to default on our personal agreements, we disempower ourselves across all the areas of our lives.

More subtle are the assumed agreements we may store unconsciously with others. These can come from a sense of obligation or what we feel we must do in order to gain, maintain or sustain the approval of others, whose love and attention we think we want. When we care enough about ourselves and our heartfelt direction in life, however, we will easily learn to risk losing the approval of other people and undertake only that which is in alignment with who we are. It is better to sacrifice lovingly the apparent friendship of even one person who disapproves of you than sabotage realizing your **Dream**.

It is vital that in order to realize the **Possible Dream** we become clear about the agreements we make, because we alone are 100 per cent responsible for honouring them. For this reason, is better to limit ourselves only to the commitments we fully mean to keep.

Learning to Live from the Inside Out

Realizing your **Possible Dream** will give you many opportunities to be creative with your life energies. The source of your creativity comes from within you. This is the source from which you will draw your inspiration, courage, strength and all the intuitive assistance and guidance you need for realizing your **Dream**. Therefore you will need to develop a strong, conscious connection with your inner worlds of awareness. Nurturing and giving time to the relationship with your inner self will also provide a solid foundation from which you can be magnificent out in the world.

Stress is actually a call to look within. Whenever our emotions or feelings are out of balance, we are receiving a 'wake-up call' to pay attention inwardly. Until looking within becomes habitual, you may respond to stress with external measures, such as food, drink or unconsciously watching TV, but instead of dulling our senses, we can use such wake-up calls in a positive way to listen with love for the cause of the upset. More importantly, we can be open to receive a new expression of loving that is pushing through, possibly in the form of wisdom, clarity or insight into our life's purpose. Have you ever noticed how blessings sometimes seem to come in disguise?

Give yourself a few minutes now to experience the exercise that follows.

Out of the Silence

Take yourself where you have minimum distraction, for example, the corner of a room with blank walls or a small dark room, and make yourself comfortable. Truth can be revealed when we 'switch off' from the world around us and listen inwardly to the gaps between our thoughts. To do this, you need to become still. You do not have to be a great meditator to do this. This is a time to just *be* with yourself, to be quiet, to relax, to breathe gently, to listen to and watch your inner worlds.

As you allow yourself to become calm, you might first notice the chattering of your mind like birdsong on a spring morning. Let it be there and listen beyond it. Listen for clues as to your purpose. Listen inwardly as a direction begins to show itself to you. Become gradually aware of where you are going ...

In the gaps between your thoughts and feelings, you will begin to notice points of light, fleeting moments of your loving, soft sounds of pure energy as you are awakened and touched inside. You may not have words for these sensations right away. Do not be concerned. Just *be* with that experience as it shows up for you.

Within those gaps you will discover your own pure motivation for loving, caring and sharing more of who you are through your life's purpose. This is your own still small voice. As you become a better listener, you will receive more of the wisdom of your own loving guidance.

This is an exercise you can do any time you feel stressed or disorientated. Being aware of the sensations of stress is an early indication that your body is calling for your attention. When you take a few minutes to stop and listen, you can 'lift away' from the disturbance and get a fresh perspective.

The door to your personal heaven of purpose opens out towards you. If you hammer on that door with pressure and demands, it cannot open and reveal itself to you. Holding patiently in quiet anticipation will in time enable you to clarify for yourself what is there waiting for you.

Gaining self-awareness in this way is far from 'selfish' in the usual limiting sense. As you tap into the power of your wisdom and love, you will be able to expand and give the best of yourself even more selflessly and effectively. In so giving, you will open to receive more of your innate goodness.

Welcoming the Wake-Up Calls

Whether we like it or not, we are living in a climate of tremendous change. Both in our own lives and in the world around us, we may notice a lack of certainty and predictability. Developments in technology and communications are changing the nature of our 'reality'. That which was once *im*possible is now possible. At the flick of a switch, we can gain instant access to volumes of information electronically that would have been unthinkable only a relatively short time ago. Mentally and emotionally, in our perceptions, beliefs and attitudes, we have yet to catch up and fully benefit from all the latest innovations. Being creatures of habit, our tendency is to seek 'security' in repeated patterns of thought and behaviour that are comfortable, so this atmosphere of uncertainty is disturbing and frightening for many of us.

However, the continuing shock of changing conditions is providing a positive wake-up call. It is a chance to let go of the past, with the darkness of its difficulties, and to make clear, positive choices to create a much brighter future for ourselves and the world at large.

Wake-up calls may come from outside us (O) or from within us (I). Do you recognize from your own experience any of the following wake-up calls?

External (O)
Job loss
Natural 'disaster', such as flood, earthquake, hurricane
Accident, such as in traffic, household, aircraft
Death of loved ones
Loss of property
Physical, mental, emotional abuse by others

Internal (I)
Disappointment in love relationship
Dissatisfaction in career or work
Loneliness

Lack of purpose or meaning in life
Feelings of betrayal, let down and depression
Sense of confusion and chaos

If you have recently experienced any of the above, you can be sure that you are not alone. But, seen positively, the climate of change is truly a wake-up call for greater achievement in many spheres of our endeavour, personally, nationally and globally. It is up to each one of us individually to choose whether to contract and hang back, wishing things stay the same, or to expand, and welcome the wake-up calls as opportunities to now make the most of our lives.

One of our opportunities today is to embrace whole-heartedly and respond positively to all the information that comes to us. Information (O) + (I) is one of our wake-up calls. So, for example, when we see a television news report of war as it is happening, or of people in some other part of the world suffering deprivation or violence, we are touched emotionally and may find ourselves prompted by such information to help in some way those whose suffering we witness. News becomes a wake-up call to a greater awareness of compassion (I) for our fellow humans (O).

We are inwardly a mirror to every event outside ourselves that touches us. Therefore, before we can effectively reach out (O) to others, we must initially learn to extend compassion towards ourselves (I). More on this later, but first, another exercise.

What Are You Hiding?

A wake-up call is like a knock on a door that can be opened to reveal more of who you really are. This exercise will assist you to see beyond to the other side of the door and receive some of the blessings that await you as you begin living your **Possible Dream**.

You can do this exercise mentally by running the questions and answers internally, but it would be more effective if you were to jot down the answers on a sheet of paper. Do it as spontaneously as possible so that you do not think too much but simply allow the answers to spring to mind in the moment. Keep running through the questions until you reach what feels for you to be a 'bottom line' response, an 'Aha!' type of insight.

1. What are you hiding?
2. How do you hide that?
3. How does hiding seem to benefit you?
4. What would you gain by being more open?

The examples below illustrate how this might look. Remember your own responses could look very different and that there are no 'right' or 'wrong' answers.

1. My self-confidence.
2. I pretend that I am needy and dependent.
3. I create an excuse to be 'real' with people, other than just to enjoy their company.
4. More fun.

1. My sense of fun.
2. By assuming life has got to be 'serious'.
3. The idea that other people will take me more seriously and not as a crazy freak.
4. Much more pleasure and enjoyment.

1. The blessings of beauty in my life.
2. By being cross and irritable sometimes with others.
3. I get to enjoy the peace and pleasure of solitude.
4. An expansion of the blessings that already exist.

This exercise takes little time to do, so take a few minutes now and enjoy it! You will find it very rewarding and you may well find many beautiful qualities that you have yet to experience fully in yourself.

The Art of Positive Focusing

Part 1 – Yourself

Living your **Possible Dream** may at times seem a bit like swimming upstream. However, with a strong positive focus, you will be able to develop whatever skills you need to negotiate the currents in such a way that your experience can be one of exhilaration and freedom, rather than stagnation and discouragement.

It has been said that:

> You can't afford the luxury of a negative thought.
> John-Roger and Peter McWilliams

This is especially true for living a **Possible Dream**. Learning to focus on the positive is an essential discipline. Negative thinking contracts the energy available to you, but focusing on the positive releases more of your creativity, enthusiasm and intuitive ability to respond wisely to any conditions you may encounter.

Positive focusing involves attuning to the level of energy within you. How can you do this? You can start very simply by spontaneously choosing a number between 10 and 1, where 10 is a high level of positive energy (bliss, happiness or joy) and 1 is a low level of negative energy (despair, sadness or depression). Right now, if you were to choose a number to show your energy level, what would it be? Just intuitively pick a number. With this awareness, you now have a further choice: to remain at the same level or to do something to raise the score (assuming you would not want to lower it).

Consider:

Life is not a problem to be solved but a mystery to be revealed.

This approach is one of loving acceptance, receptivity and inner attunement, rather than fearful denial, anxiety and undue pressure. Even positive attitudes can be laced with unnecessary effort, difficulty and uneconomic stress! We may adopt the veneer of a positive attitude, gritting our teeth, superficially smiling and, with grim determination, exercise the force of will-power to accomplish an aim. In assuming a positive attitude we may deny, shut down or exclude the wisdom of our greater sensitivity (I).

The key to positive focusing is in learning to listen (I) to your innermost feelings with courage. A positive focus embraces feelings such as sadness, loss or disappointment as turning-points to greater emotional freedom and personal energy. So even our negative emotions can be redirected and utilized to our advantage. By staying in touch

14

with the movement of energy within you, you can respond with love, compassion and tenderness to any information your feelings have for you. This quiet attunement will enable you to make wise choices for the upliftment of yourself and others.

One of the benefits of focusing on the positive will be that of experiencing, and therefore trusting, that your needs are constantly being met. Positive focusing can also lead to greater joy, happiness, individuality, responsibility to self, acceptance, understanding, co-operation and enthusiasm. So you can see that it's worth it!

The Art of Positive Focusing

Part 2 – Other People

The greatest opposition **(O)** you are likely to meet in living the **Dream** will be that of other people, who may *seem* to stand in your way. And yet they will only be reflecting a block within you **(I)**, of which you were formerly unconscious. With a positive focus, you can change your perception and attune inwardly to the lesson you are to learn from the block. When you have learned the lessons and released the energy from that block, you will then bless the 'teachers' who enabled you to experience it.

For example, you might be holding an old resentment towards a parent or caretaker who did not give you the support you wanted and needed in your early teens. The pattern of disappointment you experienced then may have already been repeated many times in your subsequent close relationships.

In order to release yourself from the pattern of disappointment you need to have the courage once again to get in touch with the pain as you first experienced it. With a positive focus of loving and forgiving towards yourself and your parent or caretaker, you can switch the negative emotion of resentment into the freedom and joy of greater understanding.

Disappointments are often the result of false expectations. So to enjoy future healthy relationships, with yourself and others, be clear in the agreements and expectations you hold. If necessary, renegotiate those agreements. For example, a couple of my acquaintance who have been happily married for 25 years have a marriage ceremony every seven years to recommit their loving participation together.

The Art of Positive Focusing

Part 3 – First Step

Through positive focusing, you will discover that:

Everything that comes *to* you is, ultimately, *for* you.

You just have to learn to see it that way.

A first step in learning the art of positive focusing is to change your perception to meet the current reality of what is, rather than what you like to think it might be. Accepting the 'what-is-ness', the current reality, of your life is a first step towards effecting the changes you would like to happen.

What is your current reality? What is true for you right now? How do you feel? How do you feel about yourself? Love yourself enough to be clear about your feelings. Would you prefer to feel differently? How can you effect a new choice, if you have one?

16

Perceiving yourself and your life from a deep level of loving will give you insights into seeing your **Possible Dream**. There is a saying that goes:

In order to get what you want,

You must enjoy what you've got.

When you can not only love, but also experience enjoyment in all that your life is currently giving you, you attain within yourself a higher level of emotional freedom. From this perspective, you are better able to know what you want. You also have the energy available to go and get it.

Power Perception

You may be familiar with the expression 'power dressing', that is to say, projecting an external image that communicates to others that we are powerful in the world. This exercise in power *perception* **(I)** is one that can lead you to first know and then achieve what you want in the light of your **Dream**.

Cast your mind back over the last 10 years of your life and bring to mind an incident that caused you a significant negative emotional reaction. It might have been a person who let you down, a lost opportunity in your career or a financial risk that did not pay off. Bring that circumstance fully now into your consciousness and become aware of all of your emotional reactions to it.

Notice where those feelings are in your physical body. You may have tension in your neck, tightness

---

in your stomach, an ache in your back or shoulders, for example. Just observe the pain. If you could calibrate the pain on the scale from 1 to 10, where 1 is a twinge and 10 is agony, what number would you give that pain? This is just information, neither good nor bad, right nor wrong.

Our unconscious 'thinks' in symbols, hence the value in interpreting the symbols of our night-time dreaming. However, our waking lives are also rich with symbology, once we learn how to perceive and interpret it with a positive focus.

Keeping in touch with those negative emotions, now spontaneously draw a pictorial diagram that represents those emotions. Do not think about it. Simply put a pen or pencil to a sheet of paper and let it move freely over the surface. You may find yourself drawing a nondescript blob, or something specific like an arrow, a box or a tree.

When you have completed the drawing, once again spontaneously, write a description of what the drawing *means* for you. Drain the last drop of information from this symbol, so that you receive fully *all* it has for you.

Symbol A is an example:

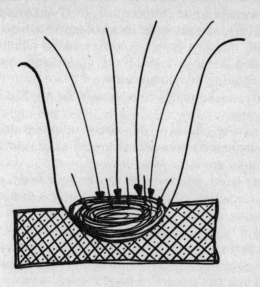

This symbol is a container that has become embedded in steel reinforced concrete. The concrete base gives a semblance of stability but it is in fact rigid and unyielding. Limited energy is going into the container, striking at a stagnant mass at the bottom of the container. Four large arrow heads are impacting from a distance above. Five smaller ones make an additional, though lesser, impact. The symbol represents the energy of anger that has become trapped.

Once you have received the insights available to you from this symbol, destroy, shred or burn the image, as it has served its purpose for you.

The next part of the exercise is to take your level of awareness to an 'impersonal' level of perception. That is to say, sense the incident you experienced as a gift that you have yet to receive. So rather than feeling that in any way it was *against* you, you will be entering your own centre of peace from which you can take an objective view of the event as being *for* you.

First of all, take your attention into your heart centre and the source of your loving. In your imagination, envisage your loving energy going from your heart into those places in your body where you experienced any tension, tightness or physical hurting. Allow your loving to release the pain, possibly with a colour of your choice, music, a favourite flower scent, heat or cooling, gentle massage or even kind words of caring to yourself.

On a fresh sheet of paper, spontaneously draw the energy of that incident as the gift it was and is now for you. Free your mind from any thinking and simply let your energy flow on to the paper with any form that emerges. When the drawing is complete, write a description of what this drawing *means* for you. Again, drain the last drop of information from the symbol, so that you truly receive *all* it has for you. Make sure there is nothing missing. You may like to go back to it in another day or so, just to be sure.

Symbol B is an example:

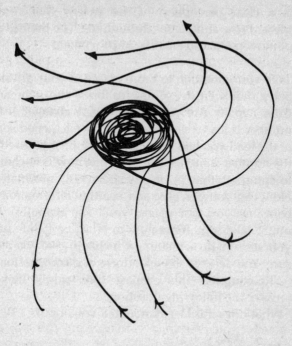

This symbol has energy and flow to it. In a way, the former symbol has been turned inside out, upside-down, with the focal point of energy being at the top. What were the walls are now three lines of energy on two sides, being drawn in towards a swirling, evolving stream of creative enthusiasm that is freely released to one side. There is a central core around which the incoming and outgoing energy circulates. The thin lines of incoming energy are transmuted and distributed with more power. The image is also that of an eye and an eye for me means the window to the soul. With the soul, there is a clear perception of the energy that comes towards me and passes through me. The themes are of movement and creative improvement.

Take your attention to those places in your physical body that were tense and calibrate the pain now from 1 to 10. Are you aware of any change? If the number is lower, you may well have lessened some of the load you had been holding against yourself. If the number is higher, the challenge now is to choose to interpret that positively. It is just information. How can you perceive and use this information as being *for* you, not *against* you? For example, you might take some time now to relax, be gentle with yourself and do something which will give you pleasure. You deserve some kindness and compassion.

To complete this exercise, you might like to answer the following question:

What does this last symbol tell you about:

    a. Who you are?
    b. The **Possible Dream** you now want to fulfil?

For example:
a. I am one who enters the flow of life, freely receiving and giving out the creative best of myself.
b. My **Possible Dream** is being one of those contributing to overall improvements in the quality of life through my clear perception, responding creatively to the resources that come to me.

You may wish to repeat this exercise with more than one experience from the past in order to receive further insights into your **Possible Dream**.

Creating your Life from the Inside Out

So far, in embarking on the adventure of living your **Possible Dream** we have been beginning to explore how to manage your energy **(I)** from the inside out. In this next step, we shall be looking at more of the concrete vision of your **Dream**, the specific focal points or objectives **(O)** towards which you will be directing your resources **(I)**. What is it that you want to fulfil?

Consider the triangle below as illustrating three main areas of focus for your life.

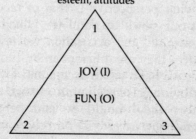

PERSONAL
Care of your health (physical, mental, emotional), values, meaning, purpose, philosophy of life, esteem, attitudes

1

JOY (I)

FUN (O)

2   3

RELATIONSHIPS
Your sense of connectedness and belonging with others

MATERIAL
Your physical needs ie. finance, job, house, car, food, clothes

3. *Material*

Many of us are accustomed to placing most of our life objectives into this area as being the most important for survival. However, in a rapidly changing world, this is the area of least security and one over which we have little direct control. Recession and the political changes world-wide make it hard for realistic, long-term economic planning. When our physical world erupts one way or another, if all our attention is directed into our material well-being, it can leave us badly shaken and feeling disempowered.

2. *Relationships*

In the past, this is the area into which many women have been educated to place most of their attention, for the sake of survival and holding a family unit together. They may have taken more than their just share of responsibility for the happiness of others, creating unhealthy dependencies in the process. We do have a degree more control in this area than in the material, though not in the sense of being able to manipulate others to fit in with what we want and think is for the best.

A more loving perspective is that of recognizing how others reflect our states of mind (I), which we can then adjust. For example, any accusation we level at another person, whoever they are, mirrors an attitude or aspect in ourselves that we have yet to accept and love. It is highly unlikely that anyone else is going to change to fit our ideal picture of how they should be and behave. We can, however, change *how we perceive* ourselves and others, and this is the area of our greatest freedom of movement and choice in relationships.

1. Personal

This is the area of your greatest freedom and choice. You *can* take better care of your health, if you so choose. You *can* create a healthier sense of esteem – again, if you so choose. You *can* also nurture more positive, life-sustaining attitudes. Only you really *know* your personal values, and what gives your life meaning and purpose. You are finally responsible for how you experience your life and can choose the quality **(I)** of well-being you want.

When you have determined the quality **(I)** of your life from within you, you can make solid choices concerning fulfilment in the areas of your relationships **(O)** and material **(O)** needs.

You will notice in the centre of the triangle **Joy (I)** and **Fun (O)**. To enhance your all-round well-being in life, you might now like to nurture within yourself the meaning those words have for you. Do you have a friend who makes you laugh? What is fun for you? Do one thing each day, simply for the fun of it. See the joy and silliness in things you might take too seriously. You can begin doing that today, tomorrow and why not the day after that? This could get to be a habit that really serves you.

Dreams – The Stuff That Miracles Are Made Of

In an *im*possible dream you may recognize a sense of *wishing and hoping*. If only, sometime in the future, maybe, perhaps – there is the wistfulness of a daydream. And we may also attach a sense of *expectation*, one that is actually laced with *doubt* about achieving the hoped-for outcome.

So, on the one hand, we have our head in the clouds and, on the other, a deep-seated fear that what we think we want, we can never really have. The result is that we probably do not get it either, but meanwhile swing emotionally between the airy 'wishing and hoping' and the despairing 'depths of doubting'. In this way, our energy **(I)** never gets properly engaged and therefore fails to be productive. Expectations so often lead to disappointments.

DAYDREAM	EXPECTATION	DISAPPOINTMENT
Wishing/hoping	Rigidness of thinking Controlling attitudes and behaviour	Low esteem

For manifesting the **Possible Dream**, however, the engagement of energy begins primarily in the heart-centred *envisioning* **(I)** of a desired outcome, as if it were already happening right now. So in place of rigid expectation is the quality of open-minded *anticipating*.

First of all we create a clear intention of what it is we really want deep down, while remaining open as to how precisely it may come about. Keeping our focus positively on the vision we hold, we keep taking the next immediate action step in the direction that leads us towards it. We evaluate that step in terms of the results it has produced for us; then choose and take the next action step. Evaluation is always positive and never needs to be harsh and critical.

If one action does not produce what we may have thought to be a 'perfect' outcome, we do not waste time and precious energy in blaming ourselves or others. We simply learn all we can from it and keep moving on. An apparent detour may well have unforeseen value, which we can receive if we are open to it.

There is a delightful aspect to anticipating and it is that of being willing and open to receive **(I) + (O)**. You never know when you may benefit from what I shall call the **Hand Unseen (HU)**.

Just for a moment, put to one side your valuable, rational thinking mind and allow yourself to contemplate the following possibility.

You are an individual, essentially alone in the world even when you are physically surrounded by others. However, what if you were actually connected invisibly to many who love and support you in your journey through life, the adventure of your **Possible Dream**? What if you are connected through your heart with many Hands as yet Unseen whose mission, delight and pleasure is to make your heartfelt **Dream** come true? How they deliver their gifts might be totally unpredictable and beyond your control. Your openness to receive is all that is required. Be prepared for some wonderful surprises.

If it is not a contradiction in terms, *listening* and *receiving* are important for *seeing* your **Dream**.

Receiving from the Hands Unseen (HUs)

This exercise is a guided visualization in which you will be allowing your creative imagination freedom from your normal restraints and expectations. Be assured that you will be using your rational mind later to consciously evaluate any insights you may receive.

As you allow yourself to touch and receive from those Hands Unseen, you will not only gain insights into your **Possible Dream**, but also the best ways in which you will be able to realize it. Perhaps the greatest challenge here is to allow yourself to be vulnerable, where 'vulnerable' has the meanings of both to be wounded and blessed. That which has hurt you in the past is a wafer-thin screen which both hides and can assist you to realize the blessings of loving that you are. To live your **Possible Dream** is to live in a greater reality of your loving and the blessings it brings to you.

You may choose to do this exercise in any one of the following ways:

1. Record it for yourself on a cassette, leaving spaces for your mind to produce images.
2. Ask someone else to read it slowly for you, in a similar way, leaving spaces for the imagery to show up.
3. Read it for yourself, closing your eyes periodically and allowing the imagery to show up in stages as you do so.

Have a notebook and pen by you so that you can record any observations from the visualization while they are still fresh in your mind.

Begin by looking down (in order to reflect inwardly) or close your eyes if that feels comfortable for you. Ask inwardly and envisage as much as you are able being filled,

28

surrounded and protected by a beautiful clear white light ... You might see it swirling around you, possibly like a delicate mist of crystal raindrops ... that freshen and lift your spirits ... Become aware of your heart centre ... and the fullness of gentle loving and beauty within you ... Notice your sensitivity ... and as you breathe, breathe into your sensitivity ... Become aware of your nuances of feeling ... like the finest threads of spun golden silk ...

*Imagine yourself being lifted higher now ... with the movement of those golden threads ... into the realms of your **Possible Dream** ... You might be able to hear the faint sounds ... the most exquisite music that soothes and calms you ... the air you breathe now feels more refined ... more nurturing ... than any you have ever experienced before ... you touch into a quality of peace within you ... a peace in which you recognize the purity of your intention ... a magnificent intention to discover more of who you truly are ... A valuable contributor in a creation larger than you ... a creation to which you belong ... and in which you are held in high esteem ...*

*Inwardly ... in your imagination ... you open your eyes ... As you look around you ... you find yourself surrounded by beings who radiate their loving towards you ... Everywhere you look ... you are aware of hands reaching out to give to you ... You hear the sounds of their appreciation of your special place here ... you feel the loving of encouraging faces that reflect a trust in you ... a powerful trust that you already have all you need to realize your **Dream** ...*

*But first of all ... they are here to give you keys to the important elements of your **Dream** ... The keys are those which will unlock the doors to your greater awareness ... your greater opening love ... and you experience your inner strength as a flame ... a flame which burns away that* which no longer serves you ... which sheds light on your about-to-unfold adventure ... and which warms you with the confidence you need to successfully meet all of your challenges.

The keys you are about to receive will reflect three aspects of your **Dream** ... the personal ... the relationships ... and the material ... So first of all ... bring to mind the personal area of your life ... your values ... your health ... your purpose ... your attitudes ... your sense of esteem ... whatever it is that now has special and unique value for you ...

You see one of these beings step towards you ... offering you a gift ... one that reflects the personal area of your life ... you reach out to receive it ... and as you receive ... you feel your heart expanding with health, energy and vitality ... What is this gift ...? What colour is it ...? How large ...? Heavy or light ...? What does it feel like to touch ...? Are there any sounds associated with your gift ...? What does this gift mean for you in the personal area of your life now ...? You place the gift at your feet as you awaken more fully to the understanding it brings you ...

This being seems to step back ... allowing another to now come towards you ... this one offering you another gift ... one which represents your relationships ... the relationships with yourself ... and others ... as you reach out to receive this gift ... you experience the delicate sweetness of fulfilment in your heart ... a profound sense of belonging in a world that loves and supports you ... What is this gift ...? What does it look like ...? Sound like ...? Feel like ...? Is it large ... or small ...? Soft ... or rough to touch ...? Are you aware of any colours ... or energy patterns associated with this gift ...? You sense a new quality of radiance ... awakening within you as this being steps back ... Once *again ... you place this gift at your feet ... where it can best support your greater understanding...*

And the next being steps forward ... extending to you another gift ... You reach out ... and this time receive into your hands that which reflects the extraordinary abundance ... an expansion of all the gifts in your heart now ready to be expressed ... your material needs being more than fully met ... What is this gift that you now receive ...? How does it look ...? What does it feel like ...? Sound like ...? What is special about this gift ...? What does it tell you about the tangible, physical support that is now available to you in your world ...? In the world of your **Possible Dream** *...?*

You place this gift at your feet with the others ... and become aware of feeling grateful for the further understanding you have received ... At your feet is the solid foundation for your **Possible Dream** *... Without the shadow of a doubt ... you know clearly what you want to do ... be ... and have ... in living your* **Possible Dream** *...*

Now, very gently and in your own timing, bring your attention back into the room where you are, keeping in mind the gifts of understanding that you received and how you experienced them.

Take each gift and write a brief description of it, including, with a positive focus, what that gift means for you in practical, everyday terms.

For example:

1. Personal
The gift is an apple. Shiny, red – which means brightness and vitality to me. There is also a crispness, which means my ability to be 'crisp' or clear in the agreements I have with myself. It is a sweet crispness, so kindly and compassionate.

In practical terms, an apple brings to mind the saying 'An apple a day, keeps the doctor away.' That does not mean I have to be eating apples every day but that each day I take time to look after my health and well-being and honour my values, integrity, sense of esteem and positive attitudes – making a daily commitment to taking care of myself.

2. Relationships

The gift is a shoe. It is gold, soft leather, newish, inviting. This, and my relationships, support my greater understanding about myself. Gold is the purest energy of loving for me, and that is what I have in relationships with myself and others. My relationships assist me to recognize the 'gold' in my consciousness because they reflect my loving towards myself. I give to myself the very best quality in the relationships I choose to sustain, so that I can go light-footed in the adventure of living my **Possible Dream** relationships. The shoe also means that I am well grounded in those relationships.

Practically speaking, the golden shoe reflects my capacity for *choosing only the best* for myself in the relationships I have. There is a softness in the sense of yielding, comfort and well-being, rather than weakness, in how I support myself and I attract that in others to whom I am close. All my relationships reflect the statement 'I am valuable.'

3. Material

The gift is a gold bar, but it is not solid gold. It is a chocolate gold bar. This tells me that my real wealth is not in the world; that the world can only provide a replica at best. The wealth of the world is to be consumed and digested or actually given as a gift since I do not like eating chocolate myself very much. Chocolate is also sticky when held for a long time. Material wealth can get 'sticky' in that I can get attached to things of the world. Then they lose their intrinsic value for me and become a messy burden. There is also something fun about a chocolate gold bar. Material things are not to be taken too seriously. They are to be enjoyed, bought, sold and passed on.

Practically, the gold bar reminds me that I am a free spirit – free to come and go materially, not to be inhibited by material assets, and open to receive all that I need. I enjoy what I have and I am free to give as I wish. Abundance in the material sense is pure joy for me. It also reflects the gold in my consciousness so that materially, I give and receive the best quality that I know, the best of my loving, with a high level of personal integrity in all I do in the world. The gift of giving is a very important, perhaps the most important, aspect of my material world.

Take some time now yourself to receive all you can from the gifts you were given by those Hands Unseen. What if at all times we were surrounded by this willingness to assist us, in ways that go far beyond the reaches of our imagination? You might like to contemplate that the HUs are always there for you. All you have to do is ask and then be open to receive. You might just find that 'miracles' become the natural order of your day!

Feeling Worthy of Receiving your Dream

Many of us do not dare to dream because we have lost contact with our intrinsic self-worth. We may get stuck in the groove of former experiences of failure and disappointment, deepened with self-blame and punishment. For example, repeated failures at dieting or giving up some addiction, such as smoking or alcohol abuse; ongoing patterns of emotional violation in relationships; refusal to deal with debt and to become financially accountable.

By reconnecting with our inherent goodness, we can lift above the grooves and see the **Possible Dream** that will make our lives fully worthwhile and delightful. The American National Association for Self Esteem (NASE) has defined a healthy self esteem as:

> The experience of being capable of meeting life's challenges and worthy of happiness.

One of the most insidious grooves we may get stuck in is that of a sense of shame about who we are, because shame becomes deeply buried in our unconscious selves. Shame is the groove that has 'I must be a bad person' written along it. That is a lie, because none of us is inherently 'bad'. Unconsciously living that lie badly distorts our self-expression and experience of life. Yet that limiting belief is almost impossible to bring to the surface because it really hurts. Shame is so painful because it destructively denies the very essence of loving that we are.

Much time, energy and, come to think of it, money can be invested in analysing grooves: where they came from and how, the nuances and variable patterns of the 'grooviness' and so forth, none of which necessarily removes you from

34

them. In fact, the more you focus on a restriction, the more it will stick to you.

A wiser approach, in relation to releasing yourself from shame, is to keep affirming the experience of esteem you want. Pay attention to and keep to the positive focus of your goodness. Then, when the time is best for you, a flash of insight will make you aware of the source of your shame. With a healthy sense of esteem, you will have the love to dismiss the shame as being unreal and will be able to free yourself to use more of your energy to fulfil your **Dream**.

Choosing your Grooves

Given that it can be helpful to have a certain track along which we can move in our lives, we may as well make it a good one that supports us. Such a track need not be restricting – a track of healthy esteem can have inbuilt flexibility, provided we honour our personal integrity.

In order to lay in the track of this reality for yourself, you will be repeating the following statement above 1,000 times:

I am lovable and capable.

Do not be concerned that, if in this precise instant, the statement does not *seem* to apply to you. If not, it is probably a truth you would *like* to experience, isn't it?

Repeating the statement may sound daunting and time-consuming. In practice, it is not. It may take 30 minutes at most. You can get into a relaxing rhythm, making check marks as described below, and will find the time goes very quickly. If you are not able to do it right now, do it tonight before you go to sleep. You will like the results. You may even start collapsing with laughter after only a few repetitions. Seeing the silly side may be what you need from the exercise.

Take a pad of paper and a pen. Each time you repeat the statement, either inwardly to yourself or out aloud if this is possible, you will draw a stroke on the page. When you have drawn four of them, strike them through with a line, making five. On each line you will have 20 repetitions. Five lines of 20 repetitions make 100. Ten chunks of 100 repetitions will take you to 1,000. Now of course you may well have a better way of chalking up 1,000 repetitions but here is one that does work. Your page will look something like this:

I am lovable and capable.

＃＃＃＃	20	
＃＃＃＃	40	
＃＃＃＃	60	
＃＃＃＃	80	
＃＃＃＃	100	100
＃＃＃＃	120	
＃＃＃＃	140	
＃＃＃＃	160	
＃＃＃＃	180	
＃＃＃＃	200	220

╫╫ ╫╫ ╫╫ ╫╫	220
╫╫ ╫╫ ╫╫ ╫╫	240
╫╫ ╫╫ ╫╫ ╫╫	260
╫╫ ╫╫ ╫╫ ╫╫	280
╫╫ ╫╫ ╫╫ ╫╫	300 300

etc to 1,000

Have fun with this one! Do it now – or make an important date with yourself and allow yourself 30 nurturing minutes.

Your 20-Year Vision

If you don't know where you're going, you will end up somewhere else.

Anon

Were you to look back over the last 20 years of your life (if you have lived that long!), you would probably see tremendous changes in your outlook, beliefs and priorities. How old were you 20 years ago? What year was it? How were you spending your time? What was most important to you – and how did you fulfil that? Who were your friends at that time? How were you getting on with your family members? Did you have any dreams at that time? And have any of them now been realized?

What if the **Possible Dream** you dream today could be realized within the next 20 years? This may seem a long time. However, often we defeat ourselves by wanting to

37

accomplish too much too soon, getting discouraged and giving up. This can create an in-built pattern of failure. Yet so many of our prayers could have been answered, had we only demonstrated patience and endurance.

In the exercise which follows, we will be looking at specific, tangible results or positive, realizable outcomes that you, as the Superyou you are, will be bringing about. The clear vision of your **Possible Dream** is important. Equally so are the unfailingly robust actions that you will be taking from one moment, one day, one week, month and year to the next to translate the vision into reality.

So what is the very best you would like for yourself in the personal, relationship and material areas of your life? Is it spiritual enlightenment? Radiantly good health? Confidence and freedom to enjoy all of your life to the full? Closeness, passion, loving sex and wonderful compatibility in your marriage partnership? Being surrounded by friends who bring you only joy, fun and great happiness? Encouraging others to take charge of their own lives? Hospice care for all those in need in your community? Changing the political structure of your country to best serve its present needs? Becoming minister for health, education or finance? Your first opera performed in New York, London or Vienna? International recognition for your work to end famine in the world? The Nobel Peace Prize for your contribution to scientific advancement?

Yes, what is your idea of heaven on earth? What is your **Possible Dream**?

Imagining Heaven on Earth

Seeing your Possible Dream

What would have to happen to make this world heaven on earth for you? What would most warm your heart and make you feel that your life is truly worthwhile, a wonderful adventure to be living? It is in your heart that you will see and recognize the **Dream**.

In case you are not familiar with 'mind-mapping', a mind-map is an effective of way of bringing to the surface information within you that you may not be aware of, by using the way the mind thinks by association. As you write it down, one thought can trigger the next until you have a design for whatever theme you may be exploring.

Draw a heart shape and in the middle write:

MY POSSIBLE DREAM

Desired Outcomes

2016 (or whatever year is now 20 years ahead)

The blank or open heart is like a clean canvas on which you can begin painting your **Possible Dream**. Choose the colours, forms, images or textures that your **Dream** will take. You might like to go back to and reflect on the exercises you have done so far in this chapter for any insights they gave you. Important also will be making contact, however you best do this, with the loving energy of your heart and the inspiration you can receive through it. Expand beyond your boundaries. Be free – have fun!

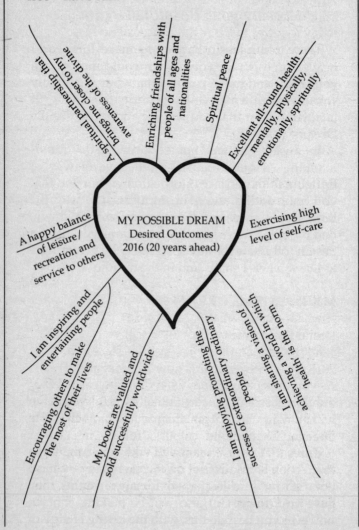

Enriching friendships with people of all ages and nationalities

Spiritual peace

A spiritual partnership that brings me closer to my awareness of the divine

Excellent all-round health – mentally, physically, emotionally, spiritually

MY POSSIBLE DREAM
Desired Outcomes
2016 (20 years ahead)

Exercising high level of self-care

A happy balance of leisure / recreation and service to others

I am inspiring and entertaining people

Encouraging others to make the most of their lives

My books are valued and sold successfully worldwide

I am enjoying promoting the success of extraordinary ordinary people

I am sharing a vision of a world in which achieving 'the norm' is the norm

Concrete First Actions

With any aspect of your dream that you put on your mind-map, choose one positive action you will take today to move in that direction. And do it.

These examples illustrate possibilities:

Personal
Take an extra 15 minutes this evening for meditation
Give up coffee, just for today
Write myself a letter of appreciation

Relationships
Call Mum and arrange a time for lunch
Write a plan to renegotiate my partnership with Bob
Let Cheryl know that what she is doing is hurtful to me

Material
Find out clearly what my debts are
Phone my lawyer to draw up a will
Send that donation to Hospice Care Research

As you took each action, what did you learn? What did you discover about yourself? Could you have had more fun? Was it an effort or was it much easier than you had thought?

The path to heaven is paved with small, manageable action steps. Do not delay, start today – get on your stairway to heaven, the heaven that is your **Possible Dream**.

Possible, Probable – I Am Doing It Now!

The imagination is such a powerful, often under-used tool. Every venture that we perceive as coming from human hands had its beginning in the imagination. Through its gifts we can begin to see what is possible and also how we can realize it.

Negatively oriented, the imagination produces in us the experience of fear. We imagine the worst and those negative pictures we hold in our minds produce all the contrasting sensations relating to threat, danger and extinction. When we can bring the fear into our hearts, to love and embrace it, we can transform it into creative, life-fulfilling energy. Truly, the fear is but a shadow which itself is cast because we stand in the way of the light.

We can always choose to turn from the shadows and see the light. And it is a light that will release the fears of darkness from our consciousness. Practically speaking, that involves accepting the negative, co-operating with it from within yourself, which in turn brings understanding and the energy of enthusiasm. That heart-centred enthusiasm is a powerful resource that will be instrumental in realizing your **Dream**.

Once you have connected yourself (I) to your **Possible Dream**, you begin living to fulfil it. What was only 'possible' now becomes 'probable'. As you embark on the adventure of your **Possible Dream**, you might like to consider preparing yourself for it. If you were to set off to explore some unknown territory, such as a jungle, rain forest or desert, you would probably look at all the ways you would want to take care of yourself while away from familiar surroundings. You might want to take along one or more guides. It is the same with your **Dream** adventure.

Optimum Learning Conditions

Pursuing uncharted tracks of your **Dream** will prove to be an education about yourself and your world. The best conditions for such learning are:

1. A feeling of safety and protection.
2. Curiosity concerning new information.
3. Openness and receptivity towards others.
4. Humour, enjoyment and sense of fun.
5. A willingness to take certain risks to discover the new in and around you.
6. A healthy esteem.

Remember, you have the capacity to self-direct, self-heal and exercise freedom of choice as you become 100 per cent responsible for your experience as the adventure of your **Possible Dream** unfolds for you.

Recognize that your opportunity is *now*! Welcome to your adventure.

Chapter 1: Theme Exercises
Seeing the Dream

Your **Possible Dream** will be revealed to you from within yourself. During this chapter, your main task is to listen inwardly for all the signs and indications concerning your **Dream**. You may see images that relate to your **Dream**. An image you see in the outer world may tell you something about an aspect of your inner **Dream**.

Here are some ways you might like to practise listening:

1. *Listen to your body for the feeling 'messages' it gives you in the form of tension, aches or discomfort. What do those pains tell you about how you may be blocking the easy flow of your energy?*

2. *Practise listening to people talking, with a positive focus, without applying your interpretations to what they are saying. Learn to listen to what others are saying beyond the simple verbal level. How you are perceiving others will give you information about how you are perceiving yourself.*

3. *You might like to experiment with spending 15 minutes a day listening inwardly to yourself, without any outer distractions.*

4. *Experiment in a freeform writing way, completing sentences which begin:*

   I am ...

Spontaneously, write anything that pops into mind, even if it seems totally ridiculous and absurd. It is a way of allowing deeper insights to rise to the surface of your mind.

5. *Allow yourself to reflect often on the following statement:*

   I am listening with awareness.

6. *The essential message you can give yourself during this chapter is:*

   I am experiencing self-awareness now.

'Self' in this case is SuperYou.

2

Using your Resources

Effective Self-Management

Until we actively start moving in the direction of our **Dream** we may have no real idea of the extraordinary support that is available to us to bring it about.

This support comes from within – in our efforts to overcome obstacles, we can discover inner resources **(I)** of courage, creativity and sheer determination. Often those who succeed in their aims do so less from latent ability and more from heartfelt motivation and will-power. All the talent and academic qualifications in the world do not count for much until they are utilized in practical ways.

What is more, a **Dream**, or vision, that is located in your heart seems to resonate in the hearts of others, who then lend their resources **(O)** to enable you to fulfil it. As you grow in greater attunement with what it is you are seeking to fulfil **(I)** you will find the resources you need almost dropping out of the sky to meet you **(O)**. Or, if they are not appearing spontaneously, you will find it fun making journeys of discovery, intuitively and otherwise, in order to locate them.

Practical Elements of Successful Self-Management

The six principles of successful self-management are:

1. To maintain an inner attunement **(I)** with your personal purpose.
2. To keep focusing on the direction **(O)** in which you are heading, towards your **Dream**.
3. To be willing to ask for what you want **(I) (O)**.
4. To remain dynamically open and receptive to receiving **(I) (O)**.
5. To develop an intuitive sense of timing as you progress. Your assets will have a way of arriving right on schedule, so it is counterproductive to put yourself, or anyone else, under pressure if you are feeling 'stuck' in any way.
6. To be grateful for *everything*, even the difficulties that come your way. What appears at first to be a stumbling block may turn out to be an even greater stepping-stone towards your **Dream**.

With successful self-management, the buck truly falls at your feet as the creator of your **Dream**. The degree to which you sustain your strong inner environment will very positively influence your ability to manage your resources to their best effect. Until you really start taking good care of yourself, you may not be fully aware of your personal resources, far less those that others may have to offer you.

So the active practice of a positive focus, which will bring about the fulfilment of your **Dream,** will be on the attitude and attention you give yourself. Noticing where and when you hold negativity against yourself, and redirecting the negative into positive, will make you aware of greater possibilities. Learning to accept and view your limitations in a positive light is an important aspect of positive focusing. As you gain experience at this, you will come to know very quickly how and when you block yourself so that you can switch from the negative into a positive release of more energy, inspiration and, ultimately, accomplishment.

Self-Care – Recharging your Personal Batteries

Realizing your **Possible Dream** will demand unconscious, mental, emotional and physical energy as you make the practical moves towards it. It is therefore important that you replenish the energy you use and have some means at your fingertips to do just that. You will come to recognize when your batteries are 'run down' and you feel out of balance one way or another. However, as you set up a regular programme of self-care for yourself, you will not be letting that happen, because you will be keeping your levels of energy, enthusiasm, well-being and personal happiness high and resourceful.

You have probably often recognized, and perhaps ignored, signs that you are getting over-tired. This kind of personal fatigue will show up in relationships – the closer the relationship, the more intense the irritation, upset or frustration with the other person is likely to be. Losing your sense of humour and perspective is a sure indication that you have lost a vital connection within yourself. Personal power failure can also show up in the physical conditions of so-called psychosomatic 'diseases'. These kinds of imbalances are a call from your body to listen, pay attention and care for yourself in some way.

Curiously perhaps, there is one resource or source of energy that naturally replenishes itself as you use it and that is the spiritual. When what you are doing is purely from your heart, your energy expands. So, to reconnect with your loving, or spiritual, essence is a good first step in recharging your batteries. You find your spiritual source by going within and getting in touch once again with the power of your values, what is true for you.

For the purpose of the following exercise, assume that you might be feeling somewhat depleted. This, incidentally, does not make you a bad person. We often try so hard to be good and do the right things that we punish ourselves when we are less than our best, which is like adding salt to the wound when we really need loving care, tenderness and attention.

Coming Home to the Heart

You might like to use this guided visualization as a rescue remedy – although you do not need to wait until your need has reached dramatic proportions! Have a pen and paper by your side for any observations you may have.

Place your hands centrally over your chest, just below your collar-bone. Feel the warmth of the contact between your hands and chest. Observe the quiet steadiness of your breathing. Close your eyes for a moment and take an intuitive check of your level of energy on a scale from 1 to 10, where 1 is very low and 10 is well topped up. What number are you at? Treat this simply as information.

Keeping your hands in touch with that loving place, close your eyes as you reflect on the flow of imagery ... First of all take yourself in your imagination to a warm red sunrise over an ocean horizon ... feel the warmth of the sun as it reveals itself to you ... receive its powerful strength as you breathe in its red colour ... hear the colour red singing in the cells of your body as you feel it empowering you ...

Let that image fade as you turn your attention to an autumn scene of brilliant orange ... leaves glowing their sustaining colour which permeates your being with confidence ... As you bring this orange colour into the cells of your body ... you feel an increasing quality of endurance ... the capacity you have to fulfil your dreams ... You hear the sweet music and feel the eternal rhythm of the orange vibration as it flows gently ... persistently throughout your consciousness ...

As this scene now fades ... you experience a sense of greater clarity as you bring into your view a field of bright yellow flowers ... extending as far as your eyes can see ... You notice a ripple of colour as the wind blows across this dance of yellow ... a lightness of understanding lifts within you ... as you allow yourself to bathe in the radiance of this yellow ... taking into your nervous system the freedom that this colour releases for you ... You find the freedom leading you into greater mental attunement ...

And as this scene loses its brilliance, you begin to see countryside of the most vivid emerald green ... So vibrant is this colour green that it catches your breath with its beauty and peacefulness ... As you allow your eyes to gaze over this rich view of many green textures and shapes ... you feel its calming, healing joy enriching and bringing you into balance ... soothing any parts of you that were in disturbance ... allowing the abundance of your own nature to come more fully into being ...

Gradually now you observe the colour changing into a powerful sapphire blue ... and in front of you ... you see the light permeating a cave filled with blue crystals ...

a sparkling blue that seems to ring the softest music ...
that soothes and restores your spirits ... Points of pure
blue light seem to touch those places, physically ...
mentally ... emotionally ... where you had been feeling
irritation, frustration and upset ... As the blue touches
you, so it brings you into who you more fully are ... a
radiant being of quiet fulfilment ...

... And even more fully as you notice the colour turn-
ing into the most majestic purple ... a magnificent violet
sheet of gossamer-thin silk. Feel it gently caress your skin
... See a beam of clear violet light shimmer over the fabric,
reflecting a beautiful radiance ... As you breathe into
your body the colour purple ... you feel old wounds
healing ... former hurts being lifted from you, as if by
magic ... This colour you discover to be the colour
of transformation ... where all that has held you back
in the past now dissolves ... and you are free to awaken
into your purest essence ... Any last traces of disturbance release into your greater enthusiasm, joy and
fulfilment ...

As all colours disappear from view, you find yourself
walking on the softest ground ... surrounded by a white
mist ... In the mist are tiny drops of clear, cleansing
water ... You feel the freshening effect as this mist
caresses your skin ... and that which in you was dark now
becomes light ... Once more you experience yourself as a
free spirit ... childlike ... happy in the freedom to just be ...
to move freely from point to point ... without restraint ...
knowing that there are no mistakes ... who you are is just
perfect ... a child of light ... following your heart ... learning lessons with ease and grace ...

When you want to fly ... you can do just that ... when
you want to dance ... that too ... Every move you make is
a statement of your purest intent ... You know you are

> *safe ... you are love ... you are loved ... you are protected
> and guided ... With this greater sense of who you are ...
> allow your consciousness to come back into this moment
> with a fresh sense of confidence and capacity for fulfilling
> your* **Dream** *...*
>
> To conclude this visualization, you might like to
> record any observations you received inwardly,
> especially those concerning how you can best take
> care of yourself on the way to your **Dream**.

Your Thoughts

It has been said that the mind is a wonderful servant but a
terrible master. Have you ever woken in the early hours of
the morning and found yourself dominated by the darkest
thoughts, unable to free yourself of them? In order to fulfil
your **Dream** it is likely that you will need to learn to
become more than ever a master of your thoughts and to
overcome the limitation of restricting mental activity **(I)**
which, if unchecked, will sabotage you.

Below are three approaches to gain dominion over your
mind:

1. Be aware of negative thoughts and stop them by
   redirecting your attention towards a positive focus.
2. Consciously nurture yourself on a daily basis with life-
   affirming, positive, self-sustaining and expansive
   thoughts.
3. Distract yourself from any negative thinking with
   humour.

In time, with the practice of these three approaches,

your sensitivity will increase in such a way that negative thinking will seem almost toxic to you. This is perhaps the good news *and* the bad news. For when you are training yourself to release negative patterns and to think positively, it can become difficult, even painful, to be with others who indulge in a limited outlook on life. Unless you have a well-developed sense of humour, that is. Well, if you do not yet have a sufficiently well-developed sense of humour, this could be your chance to develop one!

'Well-developed' is the operative expression here. Often we can see the humour in situations when sufficient time has passed and distance gives us the objectivity and perspective to 'see the funny side'. However, time here is a bit of a luxury. To progress smoothly towards your **Dream**, the sooner you can learn to recognize the ridiculous the instant it happens, the freer you can be to fulfil your vision.

Developing that essential sense of humour starts within yourself. After all, if you cannot apply humour to yourself **(I)**, you cannot really expect to apply it effectively to situations outside yourself **(O)**.

Choosing Humour – When the Choice Is Not Obvious

What is your most significant emotional block? Are you a person who easily feels angry? Or are you more prone to feeling depression? Do your excessive commitments overwhelm you at times? Do you ever find yourself caught in a dilemma when faced with difficult choices? Are you aware of when you feel fear? What emotion most traps you and in what situations?

Humour is a great key to unlocking blocked emotions. You have probably experienced how an unexpected piece of good news can lift you out of a feeling of sadness or depression. Humour can do the same. We can train ourselves in various ways to lift ourselves out of a contracted view of life and up into a more expanded view – either instantly or just as soon as we are aware of our negativity and want to switch it into the positive. Training ourselves into a new habit is a matter of first having the information and then having the discipline to lay in a new track of behaviour, or response, in certain circumstances.

It has been said that life is a sexually transmitted terminal disease. It is true that none of us is here forever. So the next time you feel stuck, snap out of it. Take a hold of that mood and exaggerate it, dramatize it as if you were portraying a part on stage. You are no longer a victim. You can now take charge of that negativity and change it when you wish. Click your fingers. Click your heels. Do it until you switch into a new perspective. Recall an incident you found funny and go over the details of it once again.

Confronting your negative thinking on a regular basis with humour is a skill that improves with practice. It does not (necessarily) happen overnight. You may wish to nurture yourself with imagery that reminds you to laugh, such as photos of laughing people, including yourself, displayed on a collage. You could collect cartoons that illustrate some of life's funny paradoxes or compile an anthology of your most amusing jokes. Begin to create and record humorous 'wins' for yourself. On a difficult day, for example, make a point of seeing the funny side at least once and write it down. Writing can assist in 'anchoring' those positive experiences you would like to be enjoying more frequently. Yes, on top of achieving those 'wins', further anchor your intention to have more fun by giving yourself a reward for your accomplishment. You are a winner, so you may as well recognize yourself as one!

Lost your Sense of Humour?

It may be hard to 'choose humour' when nothing seems very funny to you. Sitting around, wondering about it may not bring it back – that's like just hoping to find lost keys. One way or another, you need to get up and get going or *do* something to shift your humourless inertia.

When you have lost something, say, keys, you probably go over your tracks and back to those places where you might have put them down. You could do this in your imagination or physically walk to those places to help you jog your memory. When you are lacking anything, you can always retrace your steps and if you go back far enough, you can find what you once lost.

'Lack' here is the operative word. It is when we experience lack (even in the midst of plenty) that our sense of humour eludes us. Lack is a matter of perception and relates to a limited belief we are holding about ourselves and the world around us. We were born with infinite access to all the resources we could ever need, but sometimes we do not realize it. Yet when we consider the treasure chest of multi-faceted assets available to us, more than we could use in a lifetime, then life becomes very – you could almost say gleeful.

... Well, Go Find It

This exercise will help you rediscover your sense of humour. That is an inner quality, so you will be looking within you for it.

Look down or close your eyes for a moment or two as you go over the following images. Bring to mind a dull sort of scene, grey, colourless, lacking in

54

any life or vitality. You can see some lifeless shapes flopping around. They look empty.

What you are looking at is a field of **Used Beliefs**. These Used Beliefs (UBs for short) were once valuable for you but now, in the light of your **Possible Dream**, they lack the sparkle they once had for you. They are now rather sad – and what is more, they are making you feel sad and empty because they simply are no longer useful for you. There is nothing quite so desolate and joyless as an unwanted UB.

You will be happy to know that you can trade in an old UB for one that fits you better. Pick out one of the UBs you see in the field ahead of you. Notice its colour and shape. Imagine you could touch it. How does it feel? What temperature is it? Is it rough or smooth? How heavy is it? Does it have a smell? Lick it – tentatively, if that seems distasteful to you. Does it have a taste? How large is it? Are there any other distinguishing features you notice about this UB? Imagine the UB can communicate with you and find out the purpose it served for you in the past. You might like to make a note of your observations on paper.

In your own words now, what is this Used Belief? It could be similar to one of the following:

- I can only make money if I have a large capital sum.
- I have to conform to tradition to be socially acceptable.
- I am too old to enjoy good sex again.
- Life is a struggle and it is hard for me to get what I want.
- I will be Wimbledon champion one day.

This UB has served a purpose for you because it may have given you valuable guidelines for your life in the past, possibly even protected you. For example, as a toddler you might have been told not to talk to strangers. That was fine then, but as an adult with a sales career, that belief could severely limit you.

It is sometimes hard to let go of old friends, but you know now that the time has come. With only feelings of gratitude, let your UB go now. See it surrounded by a pink light of your loving and let it fade from view. Take the description you have written about it, tear it up and throw it away.

Now imagine you can turn and face the opposite direction. You are looking into your field of plenty, a cast of characters you call your **NBs – New Beliefs**. Notice how colourful, vital and fun this scene looks. These characters are having a wonderful time, enjoying a party. There is one in particular that catches your attention because it makes you laugh. This NB seems so joyful and happy, it is almost hard to hold on to.

Notice how it moves, its colours, the freedom and fun it is expressing. What is its most predominant quality? It could be daring, ecstasy, craziness, bliss or glee. Celebrate that quality with it for a moment and allow your own humour to begin bubbling through you once again. See, feel, hear your life to be the joy it is as you listen to and receive the New Belief that this character is holding for you.

Now write a brief description of your NB. This is one you may wish to keep. Write it down in large letters. For example:

- There are many ways I can make the money I need.
- I am very happy just being free to be myself.
- Sex is great for me at any age with my loving partner.
- I easily attract the best for myself in all aspects of my life.
- I love playing good club tennis now.

Make this NB an affirmation of joy that you can nurture in yourself frequently. Above all, as you use this affirmation, bring into yourself the rich abundance of humour, vitality and enthusiasm you have in your life.

Recognizing the Ridiculous

Possibly the greatest limitations we inflict on ourselves are those of our 'judgemental' attitudes. There is a distinction to be made between discernment, or 'neutral' observation, and 'judgement'. When judgement carries with it a limiting energy of restriction, such as the emotions of guilt, anger, fear, resentment, or the kind of controlling pattern of behaviour which states 'Do this *my* way, or else', a block or separation is set up in the communication and the relationship.

When we get stuck in our own point of view, taking ourselves too seriously, we become rigid and lose sight of what it is we really want. Generally speaking, most of us want more pleasure in life and less pain. The kind of emotional blocks that stem from limited thinking cause us no end of pain, on all levels. For example, have you ever heard yourself saying that someone is a 'pain in the neck'? People become literally painful to us when we hold a limited perception of them, or judgement, that is less than they really are and at the same time remain in a relationship with them.

Neutral observation, or discernment, would give you the space to respect your differences and exercise the preference of not being in a relationship which inflicts pain. Your judgements create distance, but with the disadvantage of negativity, which will cause you some kind of dis-ease. It is preferable perhaps to choose to be physically or otherwise distant from a person than remain in close proximity and suffer the poison of your judgements.

Our inner attachments to a restricted view of life's possibilities are based on rigid beliefs, which limit our freedom of movement. In our changing world, we do ourselves a great disservice by failing to embrace, if only to appreciate from afar, the differences in the ways others choose to lead their lives. Rather than point a finger of ridicule at those who have a different set of values from our own (which we do on some level when we condemn others), how much better if we could recognize the ridiculous in ourselves.

It is possible. We can live our lives from a higher perspective where we are alert for the fun and joy of a spontaneous, even foolish (to some) approach to living as we progress 'seriously' towards our **Dream**. In fact, if we do, so much better! When we can sacrifice and surrender the limitations of lack-filled beliefs, we become more open to receive. Like you, others also want more pleasure in life and if you are having fun with what you are doing, you will draw like a magnet those who want to participate with you. So the journey towards the **Dream** becomes naturally enjoyable, because you are never quite sure when and what serendipity will turn up next to support you. All you know is that it will.

Now, how do we get from our judgemental attitudes to a more unconditional state of freedom and joy?

Let's start with self-doubt, which implies self-judgement, given that we rarely know *all* that there is to know about ourselves. Self-doubt is often deeply buried because it becomes overlaid with shame and is too painful to examine. The shame that blocks us may relate to experiences, such as our sexual or financial dealings in the past, which on some level did not feel clean to us and left us feeling hungry or needy or less than worthwhile. If we bury these feelings, in doing so we hold an unseen belief that we are not worthy of our **Dream**.

Releasing Love from a Limitation

In case the idea of examining self-doubt seems seriously unpleasant to you, rest assured that you do not have to dive directly into the zone of your most shameful secrets in order to become free. Just for the exercise, say you had one shameful secret, what would it be, what would come into mind, right now? That is *not* the one you will be exploring immediately, so you can breathe a sigh of relief!

Now bring to mind the most recent relationship in which you felt blocked, one way or another. It could be with a boss, family member, spouse, partner, neighbour or even a figure from a few years ago with whom you have not yet resolved a difference inside yourself. Now think of an instance when you

---

withheld your loving contact with this person, either out of anger towards them or withdrawal from them. What did you *believe about yourself* that caused you to create separation between the two of you?

The chances are that the limitation you experienced and acted out had something to do with lack of contact with the power of your loving, in which ultimately there is no limitation.

Recalling that instance now, take a pen and paper and spontaneously draw a cartoon of yourself holding that belief or attitude about yourself. Start by drawing the cartoon and give it a name. Even if you cannot identify the limiting belief verbally, let your drawing define it for you. The 'name' will be both a description and name. For example: Anxious Annie, Proud Peter, Faking-It Fred, Resentful Rita. It is important that you do not use your real name. So that if your name is Peter and you express pride as a limiting characteristic, your cartoon character could be Proud Percival.

You do not have to be a great artist for this to work. It could even be something of a blob, with two eyes, nose and mouth. Just make it suitably *serious*. After all, weren't you feeling pretty right, not to say righteous, about your point of view, even a little (maybe a lot) hurt that you were not being loved and appreciated the way you wanted? Write a description of how you were feeling at the time. Be as fully self-righteous as you possibly can be. This was very serious for you.

Finally, imagine the 'You Cartoon' can talk with you and find out what it has to tell you. Open a dialogue with it. Keep your questions open, allowing greatest freedom of response.

Does this feel a bit silly? Don't worry. YC has come up from your unconscious to give you some valuable information so keep an open mind – something our limiting beliefs never do for us – to listen, hear and understand the important messages it has for you.

The example below illustrates how this exercise can look.

Very Cross Chrissie

I was feeling very cross, bad-tempered, irritable and angry with the world, which had dished up two conflicting choices. I wanted the best of both and could not have them, and certainly not in that mood. Deep down, I was also afraid that I would end up with neither of my choices.

Me   What can you tell me about that incident?
VCC   What do you want to know?
Me   What would you have told me if I had been

	in any mood to listen to you?
VCC	You were pulling me in two different directions and I felt very uncomfortable.
Me	Yes, I can see that. What else could I have done?
VCC	Stopped being so demanding and impatient.
Me	But I want ...
VCC	There you go again.
Me	Well, what else could I do?
VCC	Stop taking yourself so seriously.
Me	But it is serious. Can't you see?
VCC	You are making me feel very cross again.
Me	You told me to stop doing something, but I don't know what I can do – I want something more positive, please. If only you weren't so negative all the time ...
VCC	Give me a break! I got your attention, didn't I? I deserve credit for that at least. Something positive, eh? You don't need me to tell you how to deal with a dilemma. It is easy, as you know full well. Get above it, write down all the considerations of the two or more options, choose one and make a plan to pursue it, with timelines. Take the first action sooner rather than later and get that energy of yours moving right along. Anyway, you know all of this. I can't think why you should be bothering me. You do make me very cross at times.
Me	Thank you, Chrissie.
VCC	Grrrr.

You can have a lot of fun with this exercise, so

> why not try it now for yourself? Blocked emotions
> are just your energy waiting to be released – and
> that energy can take you closer to your **Dream**.

Mary had a little thought
It's fleece was white as snow
And everywhere that Mary went
That thought was sure to go ...

... so she learnt to make it a good one.

Redirecting thoughts from negative to positive is no small
task because negative habits tend to be deeply ingrained.
Rather like peeling off the layers of an onion, you may over
time discover new layers of the same limiting attitude, in
increasingly subtle ways. It is perhaps wise to take these
layers as blessings in disguise.

You are likely to find the conscious task of switching
out of the negative and into the positive one of the most
enriching experiences you can ever have. Remember to
keep your positive focus. Rather than say to yourself, 'I
don't do that [limiting thing] any more', adopt an attitude
that is one of constant vigilance and learning: 'I am learning new ways of thinking that are more life-enhancing.' In
this way, you keep an open, flexible mind and are better
prepared to meet your inner challenges when they show
up.

Directing yourself out of what can be even life-threaten-
ing attitudes into more life-enhancing attitudes can be a
lonely business, however, when those with whom you have
been formerly spending time are not making similar
advances in their lives. What is worse, being with those

who are habitually negative in their thinking and speech makes it much harder to achieve positive change for yourself. But you can choose the support you want.

Select your Supporters

Remember that your **Possible Dream** will be happening primarily from the inside out and that as you see the **Dream** inwardly and create a strong inner environment for your vision, you will find yourself drawn towards the precise resources that will enable you to make it happen. The power of your enthusiasm will propel you in ways you could never have totally planned.

So selecting your supporters will be less a matter of going out actively to hunt for them and more one of creating an open, receptive and loving environment within yourself which will naturally attract your supporters to you. That is not to say if you sit alone at home, wishing and hoping for someone to knock on the door, they will do so. They might. However, it is more likely that in the course of going about your daily activities in the world, you will attract the attention of those with whom you feel a natural and warm empathy. *Voilà*, your supporters.

There is a process of selection you may want to exercise, however. You may find yourself attracting those who are drawn towards your vitality but who are takers rather than givers and seem to drain you. Once again, let your inner sense guide you in choosing between those who are really able to support you and those whose attention may be pleasantly flattering, but in the longer term is disruptive or even debilitating.

When you have what you might call your 'team', treat each one as if he or she were the most precious gemstone. In human terms, they probably are, because their innate human value may contribute more to you than you could ever measure in monetary worth.

Clearly Communicate your Needs

At any stage in pursuing the **Dream**, you may need resources to which you do not have direct access, either inwardly or outwardly. You may need to revise an idea or a plan. You may want some information or a contact that could give you a lead in an important direction. Whatever it is you do need may not be much further than an initial phone call away from you.

Yet, how often have we suffered by being reluctant to risk asking for what we want? Being told 'No' does not need to be interpreted as a sign of personal rejection. 'Nothing ventured, nothing gained', as the saying goes. Do you know that offering others the opportunity to give to us is often enriching for them?

The clarity of your communication is important. The best of friends and colleagues can never be mind-readers, although they may do their best to give you what they think you might want. Failure to let them know exactly what you do want can lead to unnecessary misunderstanding and a block in the flow of your relationship with them.

First of all, learn to know specifically what it is you want. Then reflect on those who may be able to assist you. Give them the opportunity to participate with you by stating as precisely as you can what you need. If one person does not come back with what you want, it may be that you did not give clear enough information or instructions. It may also be that he or she is not the one who has access to the resource you want. In which case, do not give up. Ask again, but this time ask someone else. Keep asking until you receive what you seek.

Filling the Well of Encouragement

Part 1

This exercise has to do with taking good care of yourself, so that you can help take care of others or assist them to take better care of themselves.

If you can fill the well of your own support internally, you will be able to give from your overflow, so as to enrich others in their own **Dream**s. In this way, the joy of mutually giving becomes an upward spiral into increasing life fulfilment.

You can also draw on your internal support at times when you experience doubt and uncertainty. To overcome these feelings, you can prepare a programme of personal encouragement to be enjoyed:

1. Immediately (instant pick-ups as needed) **(I)**
2. Daily **(D)**
3. Weekly **(W)**

This is primarily for those moments in everyday living when doubts may seem to overwhelm you. Check them early, for they can multiply like mushrooms in moist humus.

Your source of energy and vitality comes from what you could call the child within you. It is that child, with his or her qualities of enthusiasm, adventure and willingness to learn, play and have fun, who will respond to your loving encour-

---

agement. So if some of the suggestions that follow seem silly to you as a rational adult, remember they are not intended for you as an adult.

To assist you in coming up with items to fill your Well of Encouragement, draw that well and then allow yourself to come up with the resources that will encourage you, spontaneously and without censorship. You might put on the surface those more immediate resources for the moments of doubt. Deeper down in the well are the longer-term resources with which you can sustain yourself.

Remember that central to en*cour*agement is *coeur*, the French word for heart. The well you are filling is indeed your own heart, the heart of your beingness and the source of inspiration for your **Dream**.

The example overleaf illustrates how a Well of Encouragement can look.

Draw your own well now and fill it with all you can think of to nurture yourself.

Having randomly drawn on your thoughts on the subject of personal encouragement, choose those that you will specifically undertake under the headings of 'Immediately', 'Daily' and 'Weekly'.

The example illustrates this part of the exercise:

1 Immediately
My best immediate boost is to think of something that makes me laugh and have a chuckle about it.

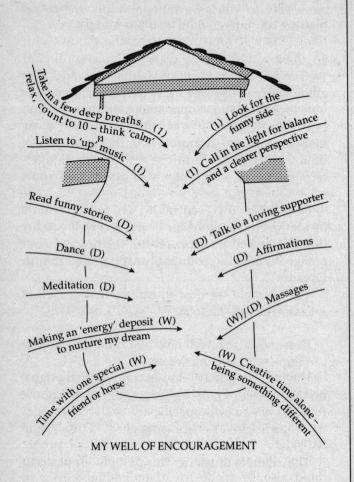

Take in a few deep breaths, (1) relax, count to 10 – think 'calm'

Listen to 'up' music (1)

(1) Look for the funny side

(1) Call in the light for balance and a clearer perspective

Read funny stories (D)

(D) Talk to a loving supporter

Dance (D)

(D) Affirmations

Meditation (D)

(W)/(D) Massages

Making an 'energy' deposit (W) to nurture my dream

Time with one special (W) friend or horse

(W) Creative time alone – being something different

MY WELL OF ENCOURAGEMENT

2 Daily
Starting the day with my meditation is the best
thing I know to prepare me to handle almost
anything.

3 Weekly
Making a point of visiting my horse and hugging
her really nurtures me and brings me back into the
softness of my heart.

To complete this exercise now, do one immediate
action, and set time aside for one daily action – to be
done today – and one weekly action – to be done
this week. Notice how you feel having taken the
time to take better care of yourself.

Filling the Well of Encouragement

Part 2

Learning how better to support yourself will give
you insights and greater understanding as to how
you can lend encouragement to those important
members of your team. The sense of 'team' here is
fairly loose. A team could be a group of people
sharing the same office, for example. Your team
could also be made up of individuals, even in
different parts of the world, who may not know of
each other but nevertheless provide significant
functions for you in the fulfilment of your **Dream**.
In the best of circumstances, any role they may play

for you is one in which they can enhance their own **Possible Dream**s. You might start by giving each one a copy of *SuperYou* as a gift of encouragement!

Above all, we all of us want to know that we are lovable and loved. Your supporters will shine with the validation you can give them for their efforts. They also need to be heard. One of the greatest gifts of love you can give is that of your time, time to listen with an open heart to what is happening for them.

You might make a point of scheduling such listening time, possibly weekly if that can be arranged, or as often as is convenient for the parties concerned. That time is for personal nurturing and involves not necessarily the tasks in which you are engaged. Think about how *you* might want to receive friendship and extend that. You could have in mind opening thoughts like the following:

- How are things going for you?
- Tell me how you feel about ...?
- What's happening with ...?
- How do you think ...?
- Did I understand you correctly the other day ...?
- Is there anything I am doing that is getting in your way ...?
- Was it fun for you when we ...?
- Is there anything I am missing from you that I need to know about ...?
- What else can you tell me that I can assist you with ...?

If you already have one or more people who are currently supporting you, take a moment now to make time to be with them, listen to them, hear, understand and appreciate them for who they are. Make a phone call now to the first person that comes to mind and arrange a time to meet up.

Materially Speaking ...

We usually think of resources or assets as being those solid objects we can touch, feel or see. They are essentially outside, rather than within us. However although the world around us is full of 'things', we can only ever use a small proportion of them at any one time. In fact, gathering material stuff around us can become a burden of repair and maintenance at best and clutter at worst.

Celebration is often associated with accumulating more 'goodies'. We are accustomed to giving ourselves material gifts for birthdays, anniversaries, passing exams and other such rites of passage. Have you ever considered celebration as part of letting go of those tangible resources which no longer play a part in your life? How would it be to travel lighter in the world as you move from one way of living into another, improved way?

Tangible resources only truly have value for us according to our ability to *use* them. Yet sometimes we cling to our possessions like driftwood in a shifting ocean. Letting go is often associated with loss and lack – and an emptiness that feels painful. So we avoid the letting go, rather than confront the hollow feeling that we dread.

There is another approach. What if, were we to let go, we were creating a space for something even better to come in its place? Must we assume that changing circumstances means that what is ahead is going to be bad in some way?

Or that we should hang on to what we have because the alternative could be so much worse? It need not be so at all. Rather than dread loss, we could celebrate it.

Changing circumstances could be exactly what is required to open doors to amazing new and wonderful opportunities which are destined to enrich and fulfil you. So why not celebrate the passing of that which is no longer useful to you, allowing a happy space within you in which you can welcome the new when it is ready to arrive?

Also, the clutter you hang on to will dull your sensitivity towards others and the priorities you need to set for yourself. 'Hang on to' is the operative expression. It is your attachments to the past that will hold you back. Those attachments may show up in many subtle ways.

Attachment to anything outside you, be it material object, a set financial income or even a person, can represent an internal attachment to a belief, pattern of behaviour or level of esteem. As we have seen, the outer world around you matches your inner state of mind. Changing your frame of mind can be greatly facilitated by letting go of what has been familiar, comfortable and safe – or at least some of it.

There may be occasions when you can rock the boats of your relationships with others and change the nature of those relationships to match your emerging new vision. At other times, you may simply have to walk away from certain people, even if temporarily, while you undergo your period of adjustment. In any event, celebrate the passing! There is truly no responsibility so great that you cannot walk away from it if you have to.

Hold gratitude in your heart and forgive yourself for any pain you may perceive yourself as inflicting. When the time for completion arrives, there is a strong possibility that the time to go different ways is true for all parties concerned.

This can be so even if it is not obvious to you at first and you are the one who has to initiate the move. It is not the physical separation that need be painful. When there is emotional separation of bitterness, anger, guilt, fear and other negative emotions, then parting can bring longer-lasting hurt.

The following exercise is one to test your willingness to let go of the past as it relates to some material object you have in your living or working environment.

Let It Go – and Be Free

Keeping in mind a NB (New Belief) from the earlier exercise, cast your mind around where you live or work and identify at least one specific object that does not fit your NB. It could be a photo, a piece of furniture, a book – anything that represents an aspect of life that is less than you now want. Intuitively, you will know exactly what it is. You will recognize it by the attachments (I) – probably sentimental – that you have in relation to the object, which far outweigh the value the object has for you now per se. Sentiment alone is costly in terms of realizing your **Dream**.

For example, if you had for years dreamed of becoming a Wimbledon champion, you might let go of a photo or a programme from a tennis competition which you failed to win. If you have been harbouring old hurt feelings from a love affair which went wrong for you a long time ago, you might let go of a love letter with bitter-sweet memories or a piece of jewellery with unhappy associations. Are you holding on to some financial asset out of a fear of impending poverty, say, a piece of land you might build on one day but know you never will? Cash it in for whatever you can get for it, and be free from it and the false expectations it holds for you.

False expectations almost inevitably lead to disappointments. Disappointments need not be part of your **Possible Dream**.

If you have any difficulty letting go, focus inwardly on your NB and how it is supporting you right now on the way to your **Possible Dream**. Set yourself a deadline, take the action required and let go! Welcome a new sense of freedom and capacity for achieving what you want. Celebrate the emerging new you!

Making the Most of your Money

Making the Most of your Inner Resources

For many of us, money is such an obstacle to deal with in life that fears concerned with it can draw us down deeply into a cycle of depression, which could cloud the confidence and optimism we need to realize our **Dream**s. The idea of 'making the most of your money' takes your attitude away from *feeling a victim* of your fears concerning money towards an abundant attitude of *feeling in charge* of your financial resources, regardless of the quantity you have. Money as a resource can be viewed as an positive asset, in many different ways that perhaps you have so far not considered.

Money is important as far as it relates to our needs and

our capacity for using it. Mistakenly, we might imagine that having money greatly in excess of our needs would in fact solve all our problems in life. In the short term, this may appear to be true, but in the longer term, another set of problems arise. The central issue to address is our attitude or beliefs about money. Money may either dominate us as a constant, nagging preoccupation or we may master it, freely and without emotional stress, as something useful for getting along in the world.

Curiously perhaps, a relative shortage of money, provided it does not disrupt our lives to the point where we become homeless or worse, can be valuable. Learning to make do with less can exercise our imagination and make us very resourceful. In this sense, a relative lack of money can be an asset.

Money in excess of our true requirements, on the other hand, can lead to *feelings of lack*, anxiety, greed and fear of impending poverty – even in the midst of plenty. It has been said that if you are feeling lack when in fact you do have all that you need, then find something to give away. If at first you cannot bring yourself to give away some of your money, then give of your time. When you give of yourself, you fill the hole of lack and return to mental and emotional balance.

Relative to your **Possible Dream**, discovering and releasing the fears you have concerning money is valuable as a step to gaining the clarity of thinking and freedom of energy that will enable you to fulfil the **Dream**. Any fears you have concerning money probably came from your earliest years of life. Basic fears relating to survival itself may have come from your parents when they were struggling to support a growing family. So be extremely kind to yourself as you examine your feelings and beliefs concerning money.

75

You can choose to switch your focus from 'money – a problem I would rather not face' to 'money – a resource I enjoy'. If money has in the past been a serious source of disturbance for you, change that disturbance now into the freedom and pleasure you can have with the money in your life, no matter how much, or how little, that is. Think of money as a symbol for energy. Learning to manage it effectively will help you learn to manage yourself more effectively.

A Lighter Look at Cash

Identify a sum of money that you can lay your hands on with which you would be willing to play and which you could let go of. It does not have to be a huge sum, just large enough to learn something from it. In fact, it could be minimal, but the larger it is the more you might learn from this exercise.

You are going to be using the money you have identified to take a lighter look at your financial resources. The fact is, your *potential* financial resources are unlimited once you are willing to ask for what you want, although the amount of money in your bank account is in a sense finite.

If you were to detach yourself from your fears related to money, or, more accurately, your capacity for receiving what you need and for expressing your talents, you could see that there is a lot of money sloshing around in the world. There is no real shortage (O). The real lack is a poor esteem (I). That which you need to fulfil your **Possible Dream** is available to you once you have clarified the details of your vision, your enthusiasm for it and your plan of action for achieving it.

What if money were simply a form of energy with which we could play? If we only had the energy and no money, how would we play?

Bring to mind one of the things in your life that you care most about. It could be a loved one, a family member, a pet animal, your work, a recreational activity, a community project with which you are involved. How can you now use the sum of money you set aside in the most creative way to support that area of your loving attention? What is the most fun *use* to which you could put the money?

Use the questions below to stimulate some spontaneous responses and make a note, even of the craziest ideas that pop into your mind. Do not be concerned if you do not have answers for each question. Just answer those for which you do have an immediate response.

- What would be the most outrageous use for this money?
- What would I do with it if I were going to totally 'waste' it?
- How would I feel if I did not 'get value' from my money?
- How would I feel if I did 'get value' for my money?
- How could I best support with this money what I care most about?
- How could I least support with this money what I care most about?

- If I were to donate this money, how could I get others to match my contribution?
- Is the sum of money I am willing to play with too large or too small?
- If so, what is the real sum I am willing to play with?
- Would I rather spend this money on myself? (Be honest here.)
- If so, how would I spend it?
- How would I play with the money and honour my esteem at the same time?
- If there were no money available to play this game, how would I have more fun in my life anyway?

Choose now how you want to play and when. Make sure you have fun, whatever it is you decide to do. Make a note of what you did, how you had fun and anything you learnt from doing the exercise.

How will you incorporate what you learnt into realizing your **Possible Dream**? Applying what you learn is an important first step to gaining greater freedom in your relationship to money **(O)** and, more importantly, in relationship to your resources of personal energy **(I)**.

Micro Solutions to Macro Problems

DEBT

Many of us have experienced debt up to a point, even if it is only on our credit cards. The amount per se is less relevant than the emotions we attach to it.

For example, as a young person, with fewer resources for repayment, a relatively small debt could be a source of anxiety. Whereas a business person, accustomed to handling larger amounts of money, could probably add a few 0s to the younger person's debt before having sleepless nights. Either way, debt is an overwhelming emotional issue when we are in the grips of it.

Nursing a debt and entertaining wishful thinking that a winning horse or similar gamble will relieve you of the issue is to avoid facing reality and dealing with it. Getting to grips with a debt, like any other apparent obstacle, can be a positively creative stimulus, a springboard that can actually assist you in realizing your **Dream**.

Get clear in your mind that you will deal with the issue, not avoid it. Your willingness alone can be the start of moving a mountain in your consciousness. Inform those concerned how you intend to repay the money and over what length of time. Get assistance with doing this if possible – there are many who have repaid debt and they can be a potential resource for you. Then follow through with what you have agreed. Keeping to your agreements is another way you will build your esteem. Renegotiate those agreements if and when necessary.

Big problems may demand creative solutions, taken over a period of time. But taking personal responsibility for your experiences and results in life, positive or negative, will increase your inner resources, while inappropriate dependency upon others will deplete them.

As already discussed, when you do take responsibility for every experience and outcome in your life, you increase your ability to respond and your sense of freedom. When you fail to meet your responsibilities, they become burdens.

So it is with money. Being 100 per cent accountable in your life for your personal energy **(I)** and your money **(O)** is a choice you make in order to be the best you can become. What you learn in successful money management you can transfer to other areas of your life. Financial difficulties can be one of those blessings in disguise.

Money – Mountain or Molehill?

You Can Move It ...

The subject of money is amazingly rich in learning for us. In this exercise, you have the opportunity to take an issue and extract the juices and joy of learning from it for yourself. The skills you develop here you will be able to transfer as a creative resource to other life circumstances in the future. You can test your power to choose between faith and doubt as you confront the issue.

Any 'problem' we have is really a *lack of awareness* as to how to deal with it. When we gain that necessary awareness, we receive a tremendous gift that may have many subsequent applications for us. A problem may prove to be an important gateway to our **Dream**. Consider that:

Problems are opportunities to grow in wisdom and love.

For this exercise now, recall an experience of debt. It may be a present circumstance or a past experience which still has lingering feelings of shame, anger, regret or discomfort for you. For the purposes of taking a new look at this issue, suspend disbelief for a short time and open your mind to the possibility that this issue, as painful as it is, or was, is right now truly a gift of extraordinary proportions.

Make sure you can be undisturbed for a short time as you do this exercise. Imagine yourself perfectly surrounded by a crystal clear white light and be aware inwardly of your loving, courage and capacity for self-forgiveness. As unpleasant as it may seem for you, bring into your mind now your debt experience. Review the following questions and write down your responses as spontaneously as they come to mind:

- What is the sum of money involved?
- Who else is involved with you, if anyone at all?
- What were the circumstances in which the debt was created? Describe them.
- What decisions did you take and make that caused this financial imbalance in your life?
- Was there any time that you were persuaded against your better judgement? If so, by whom?
- Are you blaming yourself or others for this problem?
- What were you hoping to gain, both internally and externally?
- Looking at the inner experience you wanted, have you since achieved it in other ways? If so, how?
- How do you *feel* as you experience this debt inside you right *now*?
- What are the negative emotions you associate with this problem? Describe them and write them down.

- How does this *debt* reflect your self-*doubt*? Intuitively write one sentence that describes this self-doubt.
- Seeing this debt as a gift in disguise, now switch the sentence to one of faith and self-confidence, of how you would like to be experiencing yourself and your life more positively.
- How can you forgive yourself and anyone else concerned for the judgements you have held about this issue?

Imagine for a moment that you deliberately created this debt for the very specific purpose of bringing healing, learning and upliftment into your consciousness. What was that specific purpose for you? As you receive the benefits of your wisdom, open your heart to a feeling of gratitude as it expands and warms you. Quietly, extend yourself into this gratitude. Breathe into it deeply a few times. Receive the gratitude deeply into yourself. Let every last trace of anxiety now dissolve and be transformed into your greater loving, loving towards yourself, trust in your capacity for recognizing all the blessings that may come to you in many disguises.

Make a note of any insights you have received. If the issue is one that has yet to be resolved in practical terms, choose the next, small action you will take to transform what has been your problem into an opportunity. Reward yourself in some way when you have taken the action, however small.

Listen for the Beat

Tune into your Natural Rhythm and Timing

Mastering time as a resource is one of those intangible bene-fits of inner wealth that you will be receiving on the way to realizing your **Dream**.

There may be times when you have very clear the larger picture towards which you are moving but things do not seem to be progressing at the pace you would like. This can feel very frustrating. The point is there may be more steps, and so more time, that you need to take than you perhaps had originally anticipated. What is more, those steps in themselves may become additional resources for you. If you give in to your feelings of frustration, you will block yourself from receiving what you next need. Impatience and frustration are blocks which can be switched into resources as you learn to release them. The two major inner qualities you will be developing as you master timing are patience and trust.

Time is not your enemy. View time as being only your friend. If you put undue pressure on yourself you may be a fool rushing in where angels fear to tread. Walk on the side of the angels. The secret is, while keeping your eyes focused on where you are going, to take the next immediate step in that direction. Complete that step to your satisfaction, relax a little and then take the next step.

Progressing steadily in this way, you will begin to gain a sense of 'perfect timing'. When the time is right, you may be surprised how quickly circumstances change and move and much of what you have been working towards falls almost suddenly into place. People, opportunities, events will all seem to conspire to assist you in realizing your

Dream, as you hold constantly to your vision and take each of those next steps.

In place of a feeling of frustration with the speed of events, you will develop an intuitive 'sixth' sense. Your challenge may then be one of following your intuitive guidance as a primary resource. You may feel a compulsive urge to act against your inner direction or be tempted to give in to pressure from other people to take action when you know deep down that it is untimely. Honour that inner guide. It is a very powerful resource.

Learning attunement with your natural rhythm and timing will come gradually. The experiences that work less than well for you will be wonderful teachers. This is education from the inside out because only you can ever know what is true for you. This is especially true for your personal sense of timing. Ultimately, there will be no mistakes, only experiences from which you will learn valuable information.

Wake Up!

Use your Immense Resources of Personal Treasure

Remember that your primary access to resources is from within you. You identify within yourself **(I)** whatever resources you may need from outside yourself **(O)** to realize your **Dream**.

Clearly identifying your needs is like sending out a message to whatever you seek. Next, you open to receive whatever you need. Clarifying your intention, physically moving and taking action helps what you are seeking to come and *find you*. This may sound simplistic, but when you try this approach, you may find yourself overwhelmed with the generous response to your inner request. You may well find truth in the caution:

Be careful what you ask for – you may just get it!

The point is, using your resources starts within you and moves out from you. Within **(I)** is where you exercise your choices and control. Within is your reserve of personal power with which to relate in the most effective ways available to you. As you *use* your resources you will awaken further to your own extraordinary value, your capacity to create your **Possible Dream**.

Chapter 2: Theme Exercises

Using your Resources

It has been said that if you are experiencing lack, find something to give away, because in the giving, you once again become full. Even if you think you have absolutely nothing to give, you can always give of your time. Your time is perhaps the most precious of your gifts. 'Time' here represents your life energy and fundamentally it is this for which you can be grateful. Living in the attitude of gratitude for your life will lift you into the greater perspective of your **Possible Dream**. Experiencing and expressing gratitude will assist you to disengage from the past and enable you to shift gear into the future of the **Dream**.
The following are for toning up the muscle of gratitude:

1. *Before you go to sleep at night, recall at least 10 gifts you received during the day for which you are grateful. Do this every day for one week, minimum.*

2. *Spend a day looking for the beauty around you, receiving it fully and completing the experience by spontaneously completing the following statement:*

   I am grateful for ...

If you are in an inner city area seemingly devoid of obvious 'beauty', try looking for the beauty in people's eyes – without being too obvious about it! Babies especially can give you a tremendous lift.

3. *Bring to mind the person in your life who, in this moment, you most appreciate for their involvement or presence in your life, now or in the past. Write a letter to that person expressing your appreciation both for his or her qualities as a person and whatever it was he or she gave to you. If you would like to do so, mail the letter.*

4. *Put yourself in the shoes of the person who came to mind in the last exercise and write a similar letter from him or her to you.*

5. *Take a sheet of paper and draw a pictorial diagram that represents 'gratitude' to you. You do not have to be a great artist – allow your pen or pencil freedom to move sponta-neously on the paper. Write a description of how the picture symbol illustrates the personal resources you have that will enable you to realize your **Possible Dream**.*

6. *Reflect on your life and choose the personal quality, or gift, that you most value and appreciate. The gift could be fun, kindness, compassion, caring, thoughtfulness, your sense of humour or enthusiasm. Think of the person with whom you would most like to share this gift and create an opportunity in which you can give your gift, without disclosing what you are doing to the other person.*

3

Producing Inner Power

Doing What Comes Naturally

Your inner power is the power of your loving and your capacity for utilizing it in the most effective ways towards realizing your **Dream**. It is unlimited because it is infinitely connected to other sources of human power, both known and unknown to you. You may have had experiences of connectedness already, incidences that were hard to explain, such as answering the phone to someone you were about to call yourself. It is possible to disconnect and isolate yourself from others by dwelling in negative thinking. You can also connect inwardly with those who hold you in a high positive regard and wish you well. It's your choice.

It is sometimes thought that 'God' or some Divine Power intervenes in order to bring about 'miracles'. The truth is that the experience of miracles comes from a natural way of living, in alignment with your innate positive qualities, talents and values.

Learning to live in a consciousness of miracles may be a revelation for you. Any learning best takes place when you have a healthy esteem. At turning-points in life, whether imposed from the outside or consciously chosen, as in the case of your **Possible Dream**, your esteem may feel shaken. But perhaps the best news about esteem is that there is always something we can do to improve it, however little we may feel we have. Taking steps to improve your esteem will enable you to enjoy a better quality of life (I) and with this inner freedom, you can realize your **Possible Dream**.

Until we learn our personal lessons, our history has a way of repeating itself. Feelings of low esteem experienced today may well have echoes from your past. However, knowing the reasons why your esteem might have been eroded in the past does not necessarily make it any better now. As Jesus said: 'Let the dead bury the dead.' There is nothing you can do to change your history. In any case, memory is liable to distort the facts.

What you can do, in each moment, right now, is to make a powerful, positive choice to reconnect to the loving within you and to review your current circumstances from that higher perspective. Reflect on the following 'Keys to a Healthy Esteem' and notice where you may experience a deficit. Such a 'weakness' is not a judgement *against* you, as being in some way a 'bad person'. Instead, it is an opportunity to extend kindness and compassion towards yourself in reconnecting with more of your latent inner power, your loving.

Keys to a Healthy Esteem
1. Sense of Personal Value
2. Sense of Belonging
3. Sense of Purpose
4. Sense of Capability
5. Feelings of Safety and Security
6. Experiences of Completion and Fulfilment
7. Awareness of a Spiritual Dimension

Nurturing a Healthy Esteem

A healthy, productive relationship with the world around you, whether that is other people or the results you want in your life, begins with your healthy esteem. Developing a healthy esteem is totally within your power. It is a matter of setting a clear intention, of choosing a healthy esteem and then taking action to produce the results you want. The lessons you learn in developing a healthy esteem can be transferred to creating other aspects of your **Possible Dream**.

Most of the world is not yet geared to the responsibilities associated with inner abundance and freedom of thought, word and action. There may be times when you feel like the lone ranger, pioneering in difficult, even hostile, territory. This is when you have the opportunity for healing and restoring your esteem. Like the **Possible Dream**, your healthy esteem will be created from the inside **(I)** out **(O)**.

Taking the time to develop the discipline of responsible self-care will prove probably the most important investment you can ever make. It will both save you money, because you will not be squandering your life energy with negativity, and equip you to be generally more effective and financially productive.

Turning the Keys to a Healthy Esteem

Knowing the Seven Keys to a Healthy Esteem is fine as a piece of information. However, not until you learn how to activate them, can they become a working reality for you, giving you the understanding and experience of a healthier esteem. Overleaf are some suggestions for ways in which you can strengthen your esteem in those seven areas. You might like to add your own.

1. Sense of Personal Value

- knowing who I am
- appreciation of uniqueness
- being worthy of receiving love
- self-acceptance

ACTION
- Take good care of yourself and your health – before you *need* to. Make a salad for lunch. Go to the exercise class. Snack on fruit instead of cakes and chocolate.
- Dress as good as you want to feel. Choose colours that feel good for you. Dress to be comfortable, or elegant, or fun, or even outrageous. Decide how you want to express yourself and give yourself the freedom of your self-expression.
- Are you keeping clothes that you no longer like or fit you – in any sense? Give them away, throw them out or store them where you cannot see them.
- Keep a journal to express all your thoughts and feelings.
- Validate your own experience of the world. It does matter.
- Become your own best friend. Speak kind words to yourself and establish within yourself the caring you would like to give and receive with others.

2. Sense of Belonging

- acceptance by others
- feelings of connection with family, friends, community
- intimacy and trust in close partnerships
- supportive, caring friendships

ACTION
- Take time to be with a friend who really cares for you –
  and lets you know it. Your friends are a very important
  part of developing a healthier esteem.
- Become more interesting by taking more interest in the
  world around you – people, current events, books,
  music, movies or exhibitions.
- Send bizarre or appropriate news clippings to a friend.
  Write more postcards.
- Notice the funny things that happen around you in the
  course of your daily life. Collect your own funny stories
  to entertain your friends.
- Happily receive the next compliment you are given.
  Do not automatically protest with a 'If you really knew
  me ...' Graciously accept.

3. Sense of Purpose

- knowing what I am here to do
- experiencing meaningfulness and vitality in daily
  activity
- having a positive direction in life, with clearly defined,
  achievable objectives
- motivation from heartfelt personal values

ACTION

- Make yourself a 'treasure map' of your **Possible Dream**. Cut out or draw pictures of the things you want (a home, a pet animal, a child, a beautiful garden) of things you want to do (visit Australia, learn how to sing, volunteer for a favourite charity) of words or images that represent qualities you want more in your life (love, adventure, romance, fun). Create it as a collage, add inspiring words, place it where you can see it often.
- Set small, progressive goals that you can easily meet towards your larger objectives. Make the phone call, set up the appointment – reward yourself at each small step. You will feel good, build your confidence and find it easy taking the next steps.
- View 'mistakes' as lessons well-learned. Mistakes become wisdom and are a valuable investment for the future. Your own wisdom will help prevent similar setbacks.
- Never compare yourself with others, favourably or otherwise. Enjoy improving on your own performance.
- Plan things you really want to do, people you love to see so that you have plenty to look forward to both short and long term; small and, when you are ready, large scale.

4. Sense of Capability

- confidence in achieving stated results
- knowledge of unique skills, talents, qualities and abilities
- willingness to progress personal development
- courage to risk learning new skills

ACTION

- Start each day with a vision of you doing all the right things – at home, at work, in your free time. Mentally rehearse yourself winning, just as professional athletes do.
- Even if you are not feeling confident, *act as if* you are. Sooner or later, you will realize you are no longer pretending. When you see a swan gliding gracefully across a lake, you do not see its feet paddling away at the water beneath it.
- Learn a new skill – singing, painting, jujitsu. You do not have to master it fully to have a sense of daring and accomplishment. Even learning the basics will give you a taste of success.
- Learn to do without the word 'should'. Shoulds are often the expectations of others we took on board at an early age.
  Instead of telling yourself, 'I *should* have cleaned out the garage last weekend', substitute the word 'could'. Be aware that you exercised a choice and have the option of choosing differently next time.
- Eliminate the word 'can't' from your language. Instead, say to yourself: 'I can if I want to; and if I don't want to, I don't have to.'

5. Feelings of Safety and Security

- ability to establish and honour personal boundaries
- awareness of vulnerability and need for self-care
- high level of personal responsibility and accountability
- intuitive understanding and balance in personal risk-taking

ACTION

- Let go of the need to be perfect, in your own or others' eyes. Your bullying beliefs can undermine your sense of security and attract people who abuse or threaten you. Accept that you are already perfect, just the way you are.
- Replace negative habits with positive ones. Put the money you have saved from not buying cigarettes aside for buying yourself flowers. Affirm your ability to take good care of yourself.
- Affirm your power to change, or to continue as you are. Accept that you may not be ready to give up a bad habit for now and consciously choose it as a method of coping. When you are ready, you can choose to replace the negative habit with a healthier one. This puts you in charge of your life and free to shape your future positively, in your own timing.
- Strengthen your feelings of inner power by writing down your accomplishments. When you are feeling weak or inadequate you will have a reminder to prove otherwise.
- Negative thinking, such as fearing the worst, is very disempowering. Keep your attention on what you positively want.

6. Experiences of Completion and Fulfilment

- undertaking only that which can be finished
- willingness to say 'No' to over-committing time and energy
- sense of personal control, achievement and satisfaction
- gratitude and appreciation towards self and others

ACTION

- When you have completed an objective, allow yourself time for a reward or celebration.
- Give yourself a gold star. Acknowledge your achievements and lavish praise on yourself in tangible ways. Sensory cues will enable you to close a door on the past and allow a new door to open to your future.
- Clear out your dead wood. Let clothes, household effects or other objects for which you no longer have use or value go to others who can appreciate them. Letting go of old associations will create a space for the thoughts, experiences and fulfilment of your **Possible Dream**.
- Reflect on the riches and pleasures of former events and relationships in old photographs. Think about how you might add more of these experiences to your life.
- Celebrate the gift of your life by writing a letter of appreciation to yourself for all your strengths and qualities you most value.

7. Awareness of Spiritual Dimension

- feelings of inspiration, upliftment and beauty
- joy in being alive and creatively contributing to life
- qualities of enthusiasm, expansion and passion
- finding pleasures, delight and humour in life

ACTION

- Be spontaneous. Do something different. Take a new route to work. Give yourself one day at the weekend to live fully in the present moment. Look out for the humour and enjoy just being you.
- Count your blessings. Make a list of all the people and things in your life for which you are grateful, and feel a

deep sense of appreciation for all of these good things. Know that you are worthy and feel deserving of all the good you have in your life – you are.

- Wake up happy! Begin each day in a fun way, sing, dance, listen to upbeat happy music. Go to sleep with a happy thought in your mind and the clear intention to have fun the next day.
- Treat yourself to an hour for soulful activity – a walk in the countryside, daydream time in a beautiful location, space to contemplate the miracle of your life.
- Plan and go on the heartfelt holiday of a lifetime. Choose the location and activities that will inspire you and nurture the tenderness of the special loving within you.

Appreciating your Value

This is an exercise in positive self-evaluation. You will be confining yourself to recognizing only the good within you – on the basis that what you look for is what you will find.

There are two senses of the word 'appreciate' that we are using here. One is that of gratitude, a feeling of appreciation for who you are and the gift that your life (I) represents in your world (O). This appreciation comes through knowing, from your own experience, your extraordinary value. Who me? Yes, *you!*

The second sense is similar to the appreciation *in value* of an object, such as a precious jewel, a work of art or a property. Subject to our perception, over time we too grow in value (I). Human value is in fact way beyond any possible material assessment.

You were born with an innate and priceless value. The course of your life, however it has unfolded, can enable you to recognize and realize this value as you *appreciate* each and every one of your experiences with a loving heart. The loving heart is your teacher and your healer.

Net gain: wisdom.

In this exercise, using the power of your loving heart, you will be conducting a dialogue to bring understanding to any of your life experiences so far which have been unfathomable.

Choose an incident or an experience in your life which is in some way unresolved in your consciousness. Take a pen and pad of paper and address your Loving Heart (LH) as your best friend, whom you trust entirely to confide your deepest hopes and fears, not to mention **Dream**s. Has your Loving Heart been asleep for a while? You might want to shake it gently awake. The example that follows demonstrates how this exercise can unfold.

Me   Loving Heart, are you there?

LH   Mmm?

Me   Can you spare a few moments for a chat?

LH   Where are we? What is the time?

Me   It's Thursday. Time? Nearly mid-day.

LH   Did I sleep in again? Looks nice and sunny out there today.

Me   Yes it is. Hot too. Did you have a good rest? Because I have some searching questions for you.

LH   Rest? Yes. And some pretty good dreams too. Now what was it you wanted?

Me   It's this exercise, see. I want to resolve
       something unfathomable. I am not sure
       what unfathomable really means, but here
       goes anyway.

LH   So what's the Unfathomable Something?

Me   Well, the first thing that comes to mind is:
       why did I choose to stay at school in
       England at the age of 11 when the rest of
       my family joined my dad when his work
       took him to the West Indies? I know I
       wanted to do well at school and be success
       ful in my life so from that point of view, it
       made sense to stay behind. But emotionally
       it was so painful for me and I got so home
       sick. And then I made the second less-than-
       wise decision to create a barrier between
       me and them, to stop hurting so much. I
       remember deciding never to get close to
       anyone else ever again, in case they left me.
       What do you have to say to all of that,
       LovingHeart?

LH   Quite a puzzler you have set me there. First
       of all, with what you knew at the time, in
       those circumstances, you really did make
       the best possible choice available to you.
       Perhaps to project such a choice into the
       future was less than a good idea. What
       could you learn from that?

Me   Make the best choices I can for right now
       and not necessarily expect the choices I
       make today to be everlasting in the future.

LH   Sounds wise to me. What else?

Me   That barrier I erected between me and
       other people is a real pain in the bum. I have

so much fear about getting close to people. I seem to have this automatic shut-down zone. And yet I have had lovely glimpses of what it is like to be close to someone else – I seem to get close and then I retreat in terror. So what's all that about?

LH   Are you asking me what the value is?

Me   Leading question – yes!

LH   It is really healthy to establish boundary lines between yourself and other people. You cannot live in another person's skin, nor can they live in yours. Usually it is best to establish these boundaries out of loving, rather than hurting, which is what you needed to do back then.

Me   Can I still be close to someone, with these boundary lines?

LH   Essential that you have them.

Me   Why is that?

LH   Good question. The simple answer is: spiritually, within a loving context, you are already one with any other person with whom you feel connected. One of the games you are here to play is that of learning to transcend your differences as they arise to experience the loving oneness, which is already in place. You are just not always *aware* of it. Becoming aware is a challenge – but then you enjoy challenges, don't you?

Me   So long as I can win them.

LH   You can win them – so long as you also allow others to win their challenges.

Me   I knew there had to be a catch...

LH	Yes, catch the spirit of what I am saying...
Me	So I can be close to other people?
LH	Of course – when you have a clear intention. But that is another exercise...

Be aware that in the Loving Heart is also humour which, combined with the peace of an objective view, can lead you into your wisdom.

Choose your own incident or experience to translate now into a jewel of your wisdom. Take a few deep breaths to relax yourself and get in touch with the loving within you. Have some fun with this exercise. Do it now!

You might like to do this exercise often. Each time, add to the sum of your wisdom blessings.

Feelings of Powerlessness and Lack of Control

In progressing towards your **Possible Dream**, you may well encounter feelings of powerlessness and in a way – hopefully – lack of control. A night or two of apparent doubt and sorrow is a healthy, if uncomfortable, gap and one in which you may connect to your deeper, inner power. The vulnerability you may feel will bring you in touch with the tenderness of your inner power. You may view it as the darkest hour that comes just before the dawn of a new awakening, a new life, your **Possible Dream**.

Such experiences reveal to us our true lack of control over events in our world, and other people, with whom we are close. The painful emotion of fear is extremely valuable when instead of denying or burying it, we stay in touch with and use it positively as a source of energy. Similarly, grieving the loss of a loved one, through death, divorce or relocation, is an opening through which we can choose to connect more fully to the loving within us.

Power in the world (O) is often represented by symbols, such as a sexy body, fast cars, glamorous clothing, jet-set holidays, a fat bank account, prestige and position in your local community or nation. It can be hard-edged and fraught with struggle, conflict, fear and anger. Inner power (I), however, is soft-edged. It is discovered in the still small voice of your intuition. You can gain access to its wisdom and support for you not by pressure and demands but through quiet enquiry. Like a light, it can be switched on to enable you to see through the darkness of your negative emotions. With your loving, knock gently on the door of fear and it will open towards you to reveal the light of your greater understanding.

Inner Power – Your Infinite Resource

Your inner power can be recognized in any of the following:

The power of

... loving unconditionally
... acknowledging the value in yourself and others
... forgiving yourself and others
... observing
... choosing the best available to you
... exercising preferences
... accepting life as it is
... co-operating with life as it is
... being understanding

... awakening your enthusiasm
... imagining what you most want
... creating a clear intention – your **Dream (I)**
... persisting – fulfilling your **Dream**
... focusing on the positive
... sacrificing the negative
... surrendering to a higher source
... being vulnerable and open to receive
... attuning to your wisdom
... consciously focusing on the present moment
... honouring your intuition
... recognizing humour when it is not obvious
... dreaming your **Possible Dream**

The examples of inner power above concern your relationship with who you are and are all within your capacity to direct. Developing mastership from within yourself **(I)** with your current reality **(O)** is a step towards creating the greater reality of your **Dream.**

Power Play –
Regaining Inner Control

There is nothing in your life that
enough loving cannot heal.

The goal of unconditional loving begins at home, the home in your heart. When you begin to live more fully from the heart, you will find that you will stand up more for what is true for you, and that mental and emotional separation from others is an illusion. We are all connected through the loving in the heart. When you lose sight of this true connectedness is the time you need to forgive yourself. The greatest love we can extend is forgiveness, especially towards ourselves.

Reconnecting with the love in your heart sometimes takes tremendous courage. Surrendering the barriers and controls we have set in place to protect ourselves from hurt may bring forth the spectre of those hurts. However, right next door to the hurting is your infinite supply of loving. When the time is right for you, you will be ready to see behind the protection and choose to expand your loving.

It is in the present moment that we have greatest command over our inner environment. You cannot change the thought you will have tomorrow night at precisely 8 p.m. because you have no idea what it will be. Right now, however, you *can* switch your thought into one of loving and upliftment, happiness and fulfilment.

For the next 10 minutes, observe your thoughts and feelings. Be aware of any movement of feeling, emotionally or physically, in your body. Notice how the world around you impacts on your feelings. Is it a wet gloomy day outside? Does that make you feel bad? Or do you feel happy anyway? Is there noise around you that you find irritating? Or are you simply enjoying the peace of your surroundings, beyond anything words can describe? Are you suffering the uncomfortable effects in your body of having eaten too much or having had too much to drink? Or are you enjoying the rhythm of your body functioning at a high rate of efficiency?

In the act of simple observation, there is no criticism or judgement. If you do not like what you are experiencing, you can change it. You do not have to suffer the effects of the world around you. You can, potentially, live in what might be described as a 'portable paradise'.

Forgiving yourself is the key to moving from the prison of discomfort into your personal freedom. Judgement is the jailer. So forgive any judgements you might be holding against yourself or others. You will find that forgiving is not only liberating but can also be quite intoxicating! It lifts you into the higher levels of choice and creativity that will enable you to realize your **Dream**.

At the end of your 10 minutes, repeat statements of forgiveness, similar to the ones below, to release any thoughts or feelings that disconnect you from the gentle power of your loving and inner joy. As you repeat the statements, observe how your feelings lift.

- I forgive myself for judging myself as not doing my best.
- I forgive myself for blaming myself for hurting Judy.
- I forgive myself for getting cross with the man sitting next to me.
- I forgive myself for judging myself for getting cross with that man.
- I forgive myself for holding feelings of lack and limitation against myself.
- I forgive myself for not trusting that I am being taken care of.
- I forgive myself for judging myself for thinking I am being abandoned and forgotten.
- I forgive myself for judging myself for feeling

not worthy of the love of my friends.
- I forgive myself for judging my friends and thinking they are not loving me the way I am.
- I forgive myself for judging myself for feeling separate from the people I care about.
- I forgive myself for placing demands against people and not allowing myself to receive from them their gifts of love.
- I forgive myself for judging myself as being stuck in negative feelings.
- I forgive myself for judging myself for thinking I am a negative person.
- I forgive myself for judging myself for thinking I am cut off from God's love for me.
- I forgive myself for judging God's sense of timing, etc.

As you practise random forgiveness statements, you will become more sensitive to the subtle changes that your use of language will make. It is important to be clear about your boundaries of personal accountability. You are not ultimately responsible for how others respond to you, for making them happy or sad, for example. By assuming responsibility for others' thoughts and feelings, you may be inadvertently disempowering them and yourself, rather like trying to conduct an orchestra that is in a different city from where you are now.

Remember that the degree to which you respond wisely with your inner power (I) will be equally reflected by the world (O) of events and people around you. So imagine that you are a highly attuned and sensitive electronic system that will respond most effectively to the lightest touch. What is more, you always deserve gentle, caring treatment (even if up until now that is not what you have always received).

Fear – Excitement

One Coin – Two Sides
Toss It – Or Choose Which Side You Want

As you envisage a greater reality for yourself, more in alignment with your personal values and purpose, not only will you become aware of your limiting beliefs but they are likely to assert themselves through the emotion of fear.

Fear is a natural inhibitor of change and in the normal course of events serves a valuable role. After all, if your present way of living is reasonably life-sustaining, why sabotage it?

We are almost addicted to our beliefs and to the attitudes, habits and behaviour that are supported by them. When we challenge those beliefs, we may well make a dive, compulsively, for the comfort and familiarity of our habitual patterns, even when consciously we want to make a change for the better.

For example, supposing you want to change your rigid work routine to make more time to spend with your children. Fear that if you do not stick to a set routine you might never get your work done properly may deprive you of the value and pleasure of being with your family.

One of the challenges of effecting change in your life is that it can also confront the beliefs and attitudes of those around you. For example, suppose you want to take up a fitness programme and decide to get up 15 minutes earlier in the morning to fulfil it. Fear could step forward in the form of your partner laughing at you for attempting to make the effort to improve the quality of your life. Others may not be willing to assume a journey towards their own **Possible Dream**. Their underlying fears, however, need not block you. Instead, it is possible to view fear as a negative energy which can be transformed into the life-enhancing quality of loving, to truly serve you.

First of all, it is helpful to recognize the positive purpose that fear serves.

You may recognize any one of these categories of fear:

1. *Fear of* being abandoned
   In your earliest, most impressionable years, you were absolutely dependent upon your caretakers for the fulfilment of your needs. The threat of abandonment represented a threat to your capacity to survive.

   As an adult, the fear of being abandoned might have an echo in a fear of spending time alone. Solitude may be a pleasurable experience for you. Or it may cause you to feel the desperate pain of abject loneliness, the intense self-doubt that comes from not knowing whether you are sufficiently lovable and worthy of loving.

   Self-doubt will propel you into doing almost anything for the sake of having people like you, even when it goes against the grain of your being. You may live your life *dependent in attitude* on *what you think* other people want from you. Rather than reach out and risk meeting new people, self-doubt and that fear of personal rejection may cause you to hide your loving and caring from those who would enjoy it.

2. *Fear of* losing control

As you grew up, you developed strategies to fulfil your basic needs and, later on, your wants and desires. You learnt the attitudes and behaviour that successfully enabled you to get along in the world. You would have learnt techniques from the 'gods' around you – your caretakers, authority figures, people you admired – and probably created a few of your own. Techniques' might have included temper tantrums, playing on the insecurities of people from whom you wanted something, withdrawal, moodiness and refusal to participate.

As an adult, you may still operate more from a fear of losing the control of other people and a need to employ the same strategies, than adopt more open, honest and loving ways of achieving what you want. Do you, for example, ever deny your needs and conceal your hurt feelings or concerns from a loved one by withholding your loving and not communicating, or by bullying and demanding?

Trying to gain control over others is exercising a form of power, but not the most productive. Ultimately, we can never control anyone's thoughts, feelings, attitudes and actions. Have you ever tried to change a loved one – a parent, child, husband, wife, teacher – and make him or her do what you wanted? We end up being controlled (I) by those we are trying to control (O) and limiting our own freedom in the process.

3. *Fear of* death

This fear is the most obvious to understand in that we are all inevitably heading towards death. The paradox is that we may not fully live life in all of its dimensions until we surrender the fear of death. It is when we have fully transcended this fear that we can come into a whole new way of experiencing and expressing our lives. What is more, we then no longer have the same sense of needing to control, and therefore the fear of losing control, nor do we have the same concerns about abandonment.

When we awaken to the fullness and abundance that life has for us, all fear dissolves. We discover that we are love, we are lovable and we are loved. We experience ourselves as being at one with who we are and at one with the world around us, wherever we happen to be. In that light, we know with confidence and trust that all of our needs are provided for.

The profound emotional experience of fear, and recognizing it as such, is a tremendous asset, even a 'friend', because it can be turned into a source of energy for you. It is the power of your loving in disguise. Once you accept and become familiar with feelings of fear, you can observe that energy not as a block but as a source of excitement.

The energy of fear may be exactly what you need to prepare for some new challenge in your life. It can cause you to look very carefully before you leap; to be alert and highly attuned to your environment (I) + (O). Have you ever talked in front of a large group of people or ever contemplated doing so? Many of the best public speakers experience performance nerves which are their asset for being sensitive to, and making effective contact with, their audience.

Another way of viewing fear is as a product of the imagination, directed negatively, against us. When we entertain negative thoughts, our emotions will deliver negative feelings (I). If you are gifted with a good imagination, you may have suffered the effects of negative thinking. However, a good imagination will prove a blessing when it comes to realizing your **Possible Dream**.

The following exercise will assist you in deriving benefit from your fears. Allow yourself to bring even the most insignificant fear to mind in order to do this exercise. You may well find it very revealing and useful.

Fear – A Friendly Door to Understanding

This exercise is one in which you will be using your imagination to explore a fear as though it were simply a door. The specific fear could be one you are facing right now as you contemplate the changes ahead of you in realizing your **Possible Dream**. It could equally be a recurring fear you have of a certain type of person or situation. For the purpose of this exercise, it is assumed that the fear is something you do not really like or want to have.

The door could be very small, a mousehole, for example; or it could be the door to a magnificent palace; or it could be your own front door at home. If it is small, you could imagine yourself taking a high-powered microscope to it to examine its finest details. If it is huge, you could imagine taking a step-ladder to explore it very thoroughly from top to bottom. You have no expectations about the door itself or what might be beyond it.

You might take a sample or two of the material of the door for laboratory testing. Tap it all over to listen for the density of sound – is it hollow, wooden, concrete? Make sure you get a sense of the temperature and texture by feeling it and becoming familiar with the materials with which it is composed. Be really scientific and make a note on paper of your findings. Notice any particularly distinguishing features. For example, there might be crystals or gemstones embedded on the surface. There may be a pattern or design that catches your attention.

Set out your findings as follows as if preparing to present a paper, documenting your findings for the purposes of furthering important scientific research. Curiously, you will find that as you conduct your examination, you develop an affection for this door as something familiar and comfortable. Above all, you will appreciate the beauty of its construction and the sense of safety it has for you.

My Door
Initial description
(Giving overall impressions, including size, colour, shape)
Closer visual examination
Closer sonar, textural and other sensory observations
Laboratory testing reports
Unusual distinguishing features
What I like most about my door
(Further observations)
How I will relate to my door in future
(Key: Remember to be loving)

The exercise could look something like the following:

My Door

Initial description

My door is wide, a bit like a concave cinema screen, so I have to sweep my eyes from side to side to see all of it, an arc of about 160 degrees. It is about 10 feet (3 metres) high and whatever is behind it is not visible to me, even though I am standing back from it. I am not aware of any way I can open it up to get to what is behind it. It has moving pictures on it, is quite light and colourful and in its own way entertaining.

Closer visual examination

Colours are moving over the surface – colours I really like, pink, violet, emerald, gold, electric blues. There is a rhythm and flow to the movement, a bit like a moving sea, and it is very powerful.

Closer sonar, textural and other sensory observations

The surface has a texture a bit like concrete, slightly rough, not very cold. It is thin. This door is not solid at all. As I push it, it gives way. I am aware that this 'door' is more of a screen. I do not hear any sounds on the surface of the wall, but I can hear some fun music distantly behind it. I think there are dolphins playing in the background.

Laboratory testing reports

I am apprehensive about taking any fabric of the door for testing because it is so fine I might make a hole in it. So I am not going to do any lab testing.

Unusual distinguishing features

As I look at it more closely, the 'door' has the qualities of a sail on a boat. It seems to have the

purpose of catching the wind and flowing with the currents. Funny sort of thing for a door to be doing, in my opinion. I notice that the colours seem to reflect my mood – as I feel more positive, they are brighter and more glowing. As I feel more negative, the colours become dull and murky.
What I like most about my door
(Further observations)

It is not what I expected of a 'door' at all. It is different and I like that. I have no idea how it could possibly relate to a fear, which I think of as being a 'not-good-thing to have'. I can only think that it has been designed to make the best use of the 'winds of change' which have been a feature in my life so far and which have sometimes made me fearful.

How I will relate with my door in future
(Key: Remember to be loving)

When I have those feelings I might call 'fear', I will think of my door as setting sail for some new adventure. I will keep the colours on it bright and radiant by maintaining a creative focus of positive expectancy. What is more, I will watch the changing scene as it unfolds on the door, knowing that it has taken me this far very effectively and that I can trust it to carry me forward in future adventures.

What you need to remember about this exercise is that the unconscious 'thinks' in symbol form. So trust that it will bring forward the best symbols for you to give you information concerning any fear that you have.

It is only when you get down to doing this exercise with a pen and paper that it will unfold for you. You will find it a very gentle, interesting and revealing exercise that you can do in a short space of time. So take a few minutes and do it now.

The Hidden Power in Addiction

The state of surrender to the natural flow and changeability of life is so utterly blissful. To be completely unconditionally loving and forgiving towards yourself is to experience a presence of inner power that you would not want to trade for anything. And yet in the normal course of events, we do not allow it. Getting to that state of mind – that may be the real challenge!

Becoming aware of a limitation, and switching it into something else, is what you need to do. It takes great power to contract your energy into a limitation. So when you can release yourself from it, you also release a tremendous source of personal vitality. This is the power available to you to realize your **Possible Dream**.

For the sake of this discussion, anything on which you *feel* dependent is a limitation. 'Feel' is the operative word here because whatever it is you feel dependent on is not necessarily what you need for a happy, fulfilling and successful life. Our dependencies, or addictions, are difficult to accept because they are often reinforced with shame and guilt. As mentioned earlier, *shame* is the intimately concealed fear that says:

I must be a bad person.

If we believe this, we will act in ways to fulfil it, hidden from others and often hidden from ourselves as well. To

114

admit to, and be aware of, feelings of shame is a significant first step towards freedom towards them.

Freedom *towards* those feelings leads to freedom *from* them.

Guilt refers to actions we take that do not fit some ideal image of perfection that we are expecting ourselves to fulfil. It is often identified by statements beginning:

I should have ... *or*
I should not have ...

as if an attitude of punishing ourselves for our shortcomings makes us in any way a 'better' person.

The same way as we tend to hide our feelings of guilt and shame, we deny our addictions and dependencies.

The good news with addictions and dependencies is that they have within them the seed of perfect opportunity. Shame especially is an intensely intimate feeling, if negative. The quality of intimacy can be switched into a positive feeling of well-being and connection to your inner power. Like the coin of fear, which can be flipped over to reveal excitement, the coin of shame can be flipped to reveal infinite love.

In order to receive love, as already mentioned, you begin by giving it to yourself. You heal the shame and guilt associated with your addictions and dependencies by accepting them with the power of your unconditional loving and forgiving. You may or may not choose to continue participating in the action (O), but if you do, it is as a conscious choice made with awareness (I), rather than from a compulsion which drives you.

As you produce the power of choice, you may in time discover how the dependency is serving you and the purpose it has for you. The following exercise is a first step in this direction.

Loving Discipline –
A Choice You Can Make

In your early life you may have 'learned' that discipline was harsh, that it meant being subject to punishment for non-fulfilment. What if discipline were more a way of observing your motives and actions with eyes of love to gain self-awareness and understanding?

This exercise is about learning to see and accept the motives behind a habit, without any criticism or self-judgement. If any thoughts cross your mind along the lines of: 'I shouldn't be doing this, what will so'n'so think of me?' or 'I wish I didn't keep doing this, if only I could give this up, but I can't – so what's the use?', then cancel those thoughts! Return, with love, to the process of observation.

First of all, take any habit, something simple such as doing the washing up the way you always do it and watch yourself as you do it. Do you wash the cutlery and plates in any particular order? Do you rinse them in a certain way and lay them out to drain in a regular form or are you quite chaotic in your approach? Once again, this is not an exercise in doing something the 'right' or 'wrong' way and being 'good' or 'bad' as a result. It is just uncritical observation. The first part of this exercise is bringing your power of observation to a habitual action.

Make some notes to record your observations.

How did you feel and what did you notice? Was there anything you particularly liked or disliked about your experience and expression? Were you aware of any restriction or constraint? Did you become aware of any improvements you might make to be more effective? Did your activity strike you as being at all funny – anything from mildly humorous to frankly hilarious?

The second part of this exercise is to make a change. Do some aspect of that habit or routine differently and once again observe it and how you feel about it. Often, making a change can feel a little uncomfortable, but it can also feel exhilarating and give you a shift of perspective.

The next part of this exercise is to choose a habit that you might like to change. The habit might be eating chocolates, cigarette smoking, watching TV, losing your temper or drinking too much at lunchtime. Again, this is about being loving and non-judgemental towards yourself as you bring forward your power of observation. There is no compulsion or feeling that having done the exercise, you *have to* make a change, whatever you think other people might want for you.

Choose a day to observe your habit. In the morning, as you get up, imagine a pink light around you (or another colour that has for you the quality of loving and inner strength). Breathe that colour deeply into your heart centre and feel yourself expanding inwardly into your loving. As a practice run, imagine yourself doing the habit you might like to change. Surrounded in the perfect protection of this colour, observe your habit and experience the feeling of your freedom filling and overflowing from you. This visualization will just take few moments.

Now during the day, observe when you are compelled or driven into taking the habitual action. Begin to notice the point of compulsion. Observe it. What *need* is it serving? Is there any pain, discomfort, feeling of lack, emptiness, sadness, fear or tension that motivates the compulsion? Again uncritically, observe that need and surround it with your acceptance, love and compassion and any colour that represents those qualities to you.

At the end of the day, record your observations. Notice also, if you can, when you were not conscious of acting habitually. Was there any special time, or times, of the day that the need surfaced? What were the circumstances? Were you alone, or with a particular person, or group of people? How was your body feeling at the time – tired, low in energy, nervous, lethargic?

Complete this part of the exercise with a sense of acknowledgment and appreciation towards yourself. If you experience any temptation to be critical or judgemental towards yourself, forgive yourself – *instantly!*

Choose another day on which you will respond differently to your need as it arises. As before, begin the day with a colour meditation. This time, see if you can envisage at least one alternative response to meet your need. Experience the need being satisfied and completely fulfilled in a new way. Enjoy the feeling of liberation as you experience yourself exercising a new, more life-enhancing choice for yourself.

During the day, allow yourself to experiment with one or more different responses. At the end of the day, record your observations with a sense of acknowledgment and appreciation towards yourself.

If you are at a point at which you really want to change the habit, you might like to enlist the support of a friend who can share your intention and with whom you can celebrate each small stage of your success. Above all, whatever you choose to do, be kind, compassionate and caring towards yourself. As always, your loving will pay great dividends.

Innergetics ©

The Art and Science of Positive Focusing

Every emotional burden, dependency or attachment that you have can be more than matched by the inner power of your loving. When our attachments no longer fully meet our needs, when we have outgrown them, they become heavy, like excess baggage on our journey through life. Such an attachment could be a relationship or partnership that lacks the fulfilment we really want and yet has become familiar, with *a sense of* safety and comfort. A job, even one in which we receive a salary higher than we had ever contemplated, can become a dilemma when it ceases to be fulfilling, although we enjoy *a sense of* security in the regular income, benefits and companionship of colleagues.

To let go of the outer attachments is really to surrender the inner belief, inner baggage, about ourselves that we have outgrown. You are the vehicle that is taking you all the way to your **Possible Dream**. So surrender your useless baggage, go to the petrol station of your finest love and fill up!

Letting go becomes much easier when you have a clearer idea of what you want to have more of. To get that clearer idea of what is ahead of you, celebrate all the blessings that the past has brought to you with gratitude, even glee. Everything that you have received in the past, including each breath that you have taken (have you ever stopped to think just how many breaths you have received in your life so far?), forms a foundation, a launch pad if you will, for what is to come next.

Begin right now, as you mean to go on. *Celebrate the life that you are* by ...

Celebrating the Blessings of your Past

Take a chunk of time from now back to the start of whatever career, relationship, habit or attachment you now perceive as being a block to what you want in realizing your **Possible Dream**. It could be five years in a specific career or job; 20 years of taking care of a growing family, now leaving the nest; 12 years living in a part of the world which now has more drawbacks than advantages for you. With your positive loving focus, allow your mind to scan back over those years, picking out the fond memories you have of them. Do not allow yourself to entertain such thoughts as 'If only I had [done something different], things might be better now.' Eliminate the negative before it has a chance to poison you. Remember:

> You simply cannot afford the luxury of
> a negative thought.

Recall the good times. Look for the funny side on those occasions when things went wrong and might have become a drama at the time. Enjoy this exercise! Start it today – and you may find that over the coming days, more delightful incidents will spring to mind 'out of the blue'.

As you derive more and more of the richness of your past, begin planning an event, gift or experience to celebrate the completion of that period of time. It might be a holiday somewhere special; an adventure or surprise treat with a loved one; a painting, poem or story that you create to highlight your best moments. Give yourself permission to be as creative as you can be. Your imagination is a gift that will bridge the blessings of your past into the blessings you have yet to come.

Waking Up to the Passion of your Dream

The passion of your dream rides close to the emotion of addiction, but is of a higher order in that its fulfilment has a quality of completion and does not pursue you relentlessly. The Triangle of Inner Motivation illustrates the alignment that brings about fulfilment. Mentally you need to be so *clear in thought* about what you are doing that you are able to bring forward a quality of *dedication* to your **Dream**. Emotionally, you need to *feel so passionately* about your **Dream** that you bring forward the quality of *devotion* to it. However, it is only when you take physical action to realize the **Dream** that you will come to experience its, and your own sense of, completion and fulfilment.

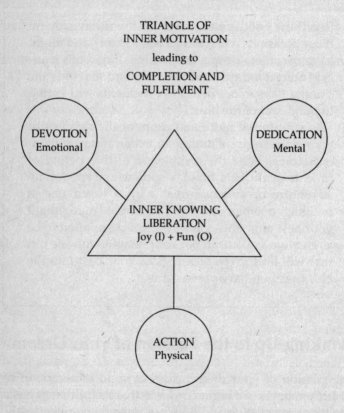

TRIANGLE OF
INNER MOTIVATION

leading to

COMPLETION AND
FULFILMENT

DEVOTION
Emotional

DEDICATION
Mental

INNER KNOWING
LIBERATION
Joy (I) + Fun (O)

ACTION
Physical

I KNOW WHAT I AM HERE TO DO
AND
I AM DOING IT WITH LOVING

DOUBT

Our human nature is to experience doubt from time to time. Like any other seemingly negative feeling, doubt has its own value. It may cause you to step back for a while from what you doing to check whether you are indeed 'on track'.

If you find yourself entertaining moments of doubt, stop what you are doing, close your eyes for a moment and become aware of the feeling. Just observe it. Describe exactly *how* it feels. What is its intensity on a scale from 1 to 10? Does it have a colour? A shape? Does it feel soft, or hard, or rough, or spiky, or prickly, or hot, or cold? Listen to it. Can you hear a word or a phrase connected with the feeling?

With a pen and paper, make a note of any observations. See how they might apply in your circumstances. Complete this line of thought by affirming, with clarity and passion:

I know what I am here to do

and

I am doing it with loving.

Repeat this affirmation last thing at night as you go to sleep. In the morning, make a note of any further insights you received on waking up.

This affirmation will bring you into alignment with your **Dream**. If you are in doubt about what to do next, stand back from your current activity, take in a few deep breaths to relax yourself and attune inwardly to the next action you can take, however small, to receive your **Dream**.

Dare to Connect to your Dream

It is one thing to see or be aware of your **Dream**. It is another to make the connection inwardly **(I)** with the energy and enthusiasm that will bring it out of the thin air of your imagination and into grounded, tangible reality **(O)**.

Excitement and daring can ignite the connection to enable you to overcome the gap of inertia. This exercise is first to awaken your excitement and daring and then bring that energy of ignition to your **Dream**.

1. Bring to mind an occasion from the past in which you experienced excitement, daring or exhilaration, for example:

riding a bicycle for the first time
taking off in a jet
talking in front of a large group of people
sexual climax

Recall any feelings of tension, fear, apprehension that built within in you just before that experience.

Notice where those tight feelings are in your body and breathe into them as you visualize the contracted energy now expanding. As you breathe out, envisage this energy completely filling every cell in your body and radiating beyond it.

Staying in touch with that fullness, become aware of the vibrant, resonant qualities of peace that signal completion.

Repeat steps 1 to 4 as they relate to your **Possible Dream**:

1. Identify one significant aspect of the **Dream** which, when it is accomplished, will bring you the greatest possible experiences of excitement and fulfilment. Bring this experience very vividly to mind. Imagine the tears of joy in your eyes, if they are there. Hear the appreciation and acknowledgment of others pouring in to you.

   Listen to your delight in simply being alive singing through you. Now, in this moment of realizing this part of your **Possible Dream**, what do you notice most clearly as your supreme gift to life?

2. Bring yourself to where you are now. What is your greatest immediate challenge that you have to take to get from where you are now to the peak experience of your **Dream**? This could be likened to that moment of diving off a high diving board, stepping off the precipice and into the abyss of unknowing, a letting go of the safe and familiar and being willing to enter unknown territory.

   Anticipate the step – and feel the energy of preparation filling your corners of resistance, building up behind the blocks of reluctance.

3. Notice where those tight feelings are in your body and breathe into them as you visualize the contracted energy now expanding. As you breathe out, envisage this energy completely filling every cell in your body and radiating beyond it.

4. Staying in touch with that fullness, become aware of the vibrant, resonant qualities of peace that signal completion.

5. With that quiet quality of repose and completion, dare to connect (I) to your **Dream**. Envisage yourself meeting that immediate challenge and successfully accomplishing it. Stay alert and awake to your opportunity. When the time is right, step forward with courage and confidence and take the action required to connect (O) to your **Dream**.

You may find it most helpful to do this exercise while making a note of each step on a pad of paper. Take your time with it. Careful preparation (I) will promote your success (O). Overcoming inertia may prove to be your greatest obstacle. Once your energy is in motion, you will become an unstoppable force of creative intention.

Clear Intention vs Will-Power

You may already be all too familiar with the expression 'The road to hell is paved with good intentions.' 'Intention' has something of a qualified meaning, while 'will-power' is often rated as a positive attribute, signifying teeth-gritting persistence and a singular intensity that brings about desired results. This approach certainly can be productive, but at a cost to personal health and well-being and sometimes to others, who can be trampled underfoot if they get in your way.

A clear, workable intention on the other hand is all-embracing. It involves having a clear vision and sense of direction towards fulfilling it. The vision-intention represents the inner focal point of *attention* which will enable you to recognize whether you are 'on' or 'off' track with your thoughts, attitudes, actions and behaviour. When you are clear **(I)** about where you are heading, then your next focal point of attention **(O)** comes as you apply yourself to the outer actions which lead to the results you want. Your will serves you when it is utilized inwardly in maintaining a positive, singular focus of attention **(I) + (O)**.

To summarize, having a clear intention involves having a singular *focus of attention* concerning your direction and a singular *focus of attention* as you take constructive action each moment to move in that direction. Instead of forging on regardless of others, you are sensitive both to their needs and to how they may be able to participate with you in the enjoyment of realizing your **Dream**. Here all parties can win their intentions, the **Possible Dreams**, they may hold in their hearts. True winning can only be a co-operative venture in which the heartfelt **Dreams** of each one of us are realized.

Creating a Clear Intention

Letting Go of the Controls
Awakening to your Inner Power

As already mentioned, alongside every relative limitation is a much greater gift. A limitation has a feeling of contraction **(I)** or stagnation to it. A gift offers unlimited expansion. First of all, you receive a gift inwardly as an awareness. Having received it, you can then share, or give, it away. In the giving, it grows **(I)**, as an experience of your greater loving. This feeling of expansion **(I)** in itself is its own reward, and no other reward need be sought. However, this is not necessarily the end of it. The gifts we freely give often do get rewarded, out of the blue.

For example, a former mechanic, who had retired, loved giving entertaining, informal talks on his philosophy of getting the most out of life in retirement to groups of people concluding their working careers. He did it purely for the love of doing what he really enjoyed. 'And,' he declared, 'do you know, they *pay* me for it as well!' What a wonderful attitude with which to *begin* any career: to do what you most love doing and, as a bonus, to be paid for it as well – and why not? It makes sense. But is it *possible*? It can be, if you wish it to be part of your **Possible Dream**.

This is where having a clear intention is valuable in creating the more specific details of your **Possible Dream**. Creating clear intentions for each stage of your **Dream** is important in learning how to make it **Possible**. Clear intentions are heart-centred. Creating them is a process of knowing **(I)** intuitively what you want, then finding how the world around you**(O)** can match your own alignment **(I)** and fulfil your inner vision.

The examples in the two columns below illustrate the difference in feeling between an open-hearted *intention* and a more rigid, fear oriented *control* as approaches to accomplishing an aim. *Grace* refers to an approach of ease, with which life can present itself as a series of blessings. *Law* implies that there is one way of doing things and there is no freedom of choice. Failure to fulfil the assumed rules of 'law' is a punishable offence and therefore instils fear and pressure.

Intention	Control
Grace	**Law**
I have plenty of time for everything I want to do.	If I work nights this week, I can probably finish the project.

My friends are always amazingly supportive.

It is extraordinary how when I need money there always seems to be more than enough.

Going to work is like taking a holiday.

My marriage is more fulfilling than I could ever have anticipated.

I suppose I *ought* to ask Pat to lunch.

I have *no idea* whether I shall be able to pay the rent next month.

Will the boss be in a bad mood *again* this morning?

I wish there were something else I could do to make this marriage *work*.

You can probably see from these examples the different *quality of energy and freedom* between the *Grace of Intention* and the *Law of Control*. Many of us have been primarily 'educated' and trained in the *Law of Control*. In the following exercise, you have the opportunity to explore and experiment in creating your own clear intentions, from the heart, as you learn to live more grace-fully in realizing your **Possible Dream**.

Recognizing the Doors of Opportunity

Your End Result Visions

Returning to Chapter 1 and the three areas of focus for your life:

1. Personal
2. Relationships
3. Material

---

what would be the one area in which to *embark* on creating your **Possible Dream**? It does not matter which one you choose. The nurturing and expansion you bring to one will enhance the other two.

So, for example, as you take steps to feel better about yourself by developing a healthier esteem, you will experience greater confidence in making the career moves you want and want to enjoy more fully your relationships with others. Choosing a more fulfilling career that matches your current aptitudes and motivation will enhance your esteem and self-image in personal relationships. Gaining greater freedom of expression in your relationships will give you freedom in those other two areas of your life.

If you have a concern about body weight or a wish to give up a smoking habit, you may wish to begin within the area of your personal development. If you are unhappy in a friendship that is important to you, then relationships might be a starting-point for you. If you are feeling stuck, bored or dissatisfied with your vocation or financial well-being, you might choose the material area.

Even if you are not clear about exactly what you do want, you probably have some ideas about what you don't want, which is a good place to start. Remember that however inadequate, unsatisfactory or lacking a current experience or circumstance may be, it is truly a door of opportunity for you to awaken into greater awareness of who you really are, your innate talents, qualities, creativity and personal strengths.

Take one specific area that you would like to envisage becoming part of your **Possible Dream**.

Bring to mind a specific step you will need to take, one about which you have some reluctance or even fear. For example, if you are dissatisfied in your job, you might look for ways of expanding your areas of responsibility within the same company before handing in your notice, but standing up for yourself in a greater way now may make you feel apprehensive. Wonderful. This 'fear' is really 'preparation energy'. It will make you sensitive to what you need to take really good care of yourself.

Consider the following questions:

- What is the positive outcome you would like to experience for yourself, having taken the necessary next step?
- What specifically do you need to *do* now, in preparation?
- How can you best prepare yourself to achieve your stated outcome?
- What support do you need: from yourself; from others?
- What would you like to receive from your close friends in order to feel nurtured? (Before you take the step and afterwards as an acknowledgment?)
- Is there anything you need to further clarify for yourself before you take action?
- Describe as fully as possible your experience of being at your end result vision. See, hear, feel yourself in all dimensions of the picture. Note the inner qualities you are experiencing, even any tastes or smells which are associated with being in the vision.

This stage is about clarifying your *intention* **(I)**, not the *method* **(O)** by which you will achieve your result. Do not get hung up on the method until you are clear about your end result vision. Similarly, do not force an inappropriate time on yourself for when you will take the action. Part of the purpose of the preparation energy is to assist you to be sensitive to the appropriate time to take action. You will know this inwardly. This exercise is a step in learning to trust your intuition, to begin living more successfully, more intuitively.

This is a pencil and paper exercise. Now you have considered the questions, start writing down answers to them and experience an inner fullness within, as you envisage yourself with what it is you want. You will discover that this approach will awaken you to a way of living that will make your life truly the adventure it was meant to become.

Revealing Yourself to Yourself

As already mentioned, before you can fully learn to master your resources of life energy and talent, you need to get in touch with and experience the power within you which naturally sustains your life. You need to know who you are. If in your chosen field of personal qualities you are truly a lion, you will never make the most of your life if you masquerade as a lamb. Figuratively speaking, you need to get out there and roar!

Who you are matters and your contribution is valuable, whether it is to your immediate family and loved ones, your community, nation or even the world as a whole. The creative input you make can potentially make a great difference to the lives of many, so do not underestimate the power you have to effect positive changes in a world which is crying out for them. When you have woken up to your innate magnificence, you will recognize that same magnificence in others and in the extraordinary world in which we live.

Theme Exercises

Producing Inner Power

When we are connected to our inner power, we are in touch with all we need and the resources with which to fulfil those needs. More than this, being connected in this way makes for an abundant and extraordinarily rewarding life. This is your **Possible Dream**.

When we disconnect or separate ourselves from this reality we have an opportunity to forgive ourselves. Forgiving is the key to reconnecting and it takes place in your heart – the centre in which you feel loving.

The following 'mini-forgiveness exercises' may assist you any time you are feeling separated, disconnected or less than loving within yourself.

1. *Repeat to yourself the following statements:*
    - At all times, in all places, I am doing the best I can with what I know and with what I have to work.
    - I am forgiven.
    - I am loved.

Take in a deep breath, relax and this time imagine a favourite colour as you repeat them again.

2. *Another forgiveness statement that can be valuable to repeat inwardly just before you go to sleep at night is:*

> I forgive myself
> for any judgements I have made
> consciously or unconsciously
> against myself
> or any other being or situation.

As you repeat it, imagine saying it from the centre of your chest just about halfway between your throat and your diaphragm. Feel your energy release and radiate out from this centre to fill your whole body.

3. *If forgiveness had a special colour for you, what would that be? Now imagine yourself being filled, surrounded and protected by that colour so that any walls of separation or disconnection are instantly dissolved and released into more of your inner power.*

4. *If forgiveness had a distinct sound for you, what would that sound be – flutes, raindrops falling, choral music, birdsong? Listen to the sounds of forgiveness and allow yourself to soar high above your hurts and into a peacefulness of the attunement with your inner power.*

5. *Here is another statement to repeat – although you may need to adapt it if it conflicts with your own religious or spiritual inclination. Get the sense of what it means for you and choose whatever words work best for you.*

> I forgive myself for forgetting that I am divine.

6. *The SuperYou of your **Possible Dream** is the inner power*

of your loving. This loving is not sentimental or wishy-washy but bold, courageous and life-fulfilling. It is also highly sensitive and attuned **(I) + (O)**.

Take a few moments now to attune yourself to the qualities of this loving. If you find there is anything standing between you and your loving, complete the following statement until you re-experience your inner connection:

I forgive myself for holding ... against the awareness of my loving.

You may fill in the blank with 'anger', 'hurt feelings', 'resentment', 'misunderstanding', 'guilt', 'panic', 'anxiety', 'depression', etc.

Complete this exercise with:

I am love.

4

Exercising Freedom

Taking a Lighter Look at the Possible Dream

Today, we are faced with insurmountable opportunities – to exercise our personal freedom and realize our **Possible Dream**s. As with any other form of exercise, it is with practice that we improve our skills. To enhance your experience of personal freedom, this chapter offers a comprehensive training programme in preparation for realizing your **Dream**.

You can start right now, just where you are. Freedom begins with a quality of relaxation and expansion. So take five slow deep breaths. Allow yourself to let go of any preoccupations you might have. Stretch your arms and legs, as you might imagine an animal emerging from winter hibernation, ready to re-enter the world in springtime. Learning to exercise freedom (I) can be like awakening to fresh vitality, available for new growth.

Refreshed and alert, you are now open to the opportunities to develop your personal capacities. The world around you is laden with gifts with which you can enhance the quality of your life. Surrender to the joy that is available to you! Remember that, ultimately, every experience you encounter is *for* you. All ways, always you are a winner. You are a winner because you will achieve whatever you choose to give your attention. If you want success, choose success. If you want love, choose love. If you want freedom, choose freedom.

You might want success, love *and* freedom and have yet to achieve them. Rarely are we educated through our school systems to give success, love and freedom priority in our intentions. Generally speaking, we are taught that academic excellence will lead to success in the world, love and appreciation from others and the freedom to do what we want. By now, it has surely been demonstrated often enough that the value of a primarily academic education has been overtaken by more human needs and considerations. Even, and sometimes especially, if you did not do well academically you may nevertheless excel in making the most of your life, *on your own terms*.

The messages you received through your formative years may have left a negative imprint that subsequently conditioned your life. There was a story told about a Texas All Star team player who was lecturing in a prison. His father used to say to him: 'Some day, son, you're going to be a star.' He asked those in the group whose parents had said that one day they'd end up in jail to raise their hands. Ninety per cent of the group raised their hands.

A classroom survey showed that typically 12 negative to 3 positive comments are given to students, but that teachers think they give twice as many positive comments as they do. We cannot be too careful about the messages we give to ourselves (I) or others (O). It is when we reinforce our value as human beings that we begin to win freedom in our lives.

Personal Freedom –
What Is It for You?

This is a pencil and paper exercise in which you can reveal for yourself the deeper meaning that freedom has for you.

You have probably experienced days when you have felt in some way trapped by the obligations of your circumstances. Perhaps you resent having to go to work to support your family – and then feel guilty for being resentful. Maybe you feel burdened by having taken on more commitments than you can reasonably handle, but were not able to refuse when asked. Or have you ever looked at your waistline and wished you could eat all the chips, cheese and chocolate you wanted – without having them show up as extra inches?

As you do this exercise, allow yourself to respond spontaneously with whatever thought comes into your mind, however irrational. This is not an exam paper with right or wrong answers, a percentage given and PASS or FAIL stamped across it. Have the courage the explore the truth for yourself as it is revealed to you.

If you really want to get the most from this exercise, make it fun for yourself. See how in the process of doing it you might awaken to more of your joy and pleasure in living. Dare yourself to be more silly than serious.

Start by reflecting on the following statement openings:

1. Freedom is ...
2. Choosing freedom for me means ...
3. If I were exercising freedom, I would ...

Think about the three areas of your life that you are now enhancing as your **Possible Dream** and how your freedom might apply:

1. Personal
2. Relationships
3. Material

Keeping these three areas in the back of your mind, complete each statement with an instant response. When you have done the three, go over them again with another set of intuitive responses. Keep repeating the exercise until you have arrived at what feels like a 'bottom line' for you.

For example:

1. Freedom is walking briskly in the fresh air on a beach.
2. Choosing freedom for me means not having feelings of obligation weighing me down.
3. If I were exercising freedom, I would have a lot of fun breaking all the silly rules I have given myself about what it takes to be successful.

1. Freedom is peace of mind.
2. Choosing freedom for me means giving those I love the time and space to be the best they can become.
3. If I were exercising freedom, I would trust my intuition much more.

1. Freedom is loving myself and others.
2. Choosing freedom for me means remembering to focus on the best in myself and others.
3. If I were exercising freedom, I would recognize my greatest talents and use them to assist others.

1. Freedom is taking time every day for my meditation.
2. Choosing freedom for me means daring to be outrageous.
3. If I were exercising freedom, I would write the letter I have been putting off doing.

You may become aware of your patterns of rebellion. As you were growing up, you may have given up your personal freedom to some outer authority, parent, teacher or state official, with a sense of resignation. Or you might have fought it and be fighting it still. Either way, there is no real freedom in fighting *against* a person, real or imaginary. Standing up *for* what you want is another matter. More of that later. Now is the time you can claim authority over your own life with greater freedom and personal accountability.

To complete this exercise, notice what you learnt and whether there is any action you wish to take. You might wish to record your observations in a journal.

Receiving the Keys to your Freedom

As described in the last chapter, our addictions, obsessions, compulsions and aversions are driven by our fears:

a.   a fear of the unknown future
b.   a fear of being abandoned
c.   a fear of losing control of the events and
     people around us
d.   a fear of getting in touch with our deepest feelings of
     love

The following keys will assist you in seeing how you can turn these fears into greater experiences of freedom.

1. **Warrior of Awareness**
    Living in the present moment.
2. **Holy – or Lonely?**
    Physically **(O)** we may be alone. Spiritually **(I)** we never are.
    Loneliness is a choice we need not make.
3. **Choosing Freedom – All the Way to Liberation**
    Freedom is a choice **(I)**.
4. **Grieving the Past**
    Awaken in grace to a new dimension of your loving and joy.

Warrior of Awareness

DON'T WORRY – BE HAPPY!
Now is the only moment in which to practise freedom, to exercise your intention to be free. If an issue is concerning

141

you, do something about it – *now*! Make the issues **(I)** + **(O)** in your life a priority and clear them up so you can get on with what you want.

A warrior generally has the image of being a fighter **(O)**, combating a territorial enemy. To prepare for battle, he or she gets fit and learns to co-operate as a disciplined member of a team so that, together with others, he or she can achieve a stated objective: generally, annihilation, one way or another, of the enemy.

We are now seeing military training being directed for 'peace-keeping' purposes, even, where possible, food distribution. There is a subtle but distinct shift of purpose from being *against* an enemy to being *for* the continuation of a happy co-existence. Similar discipline, different intention. We may not yet be expert at this role, but then some miracles do not take place overnight. It is worth remembering that new skills take practice to perfect.

The subtle enemy of your **Possible Dream** is worry. Worry is often no more than a concern related to lack of information about the future. You might like to feel in control of life. Good luck! Yes, it can be scary to sacrifice the feeling that you are in control and to let go of the habits that perpetuate that particular illusion. Do you remember the *fears* of being abandoned and of losing control from the last chapter? The way out of limiting habit patterns is by developing the *faith* and *trust* that you are never abandoned, that 'life' takes care of you very abundantly and therefore, you do not need to *feel* in control. *Faith* and *trust* are two of the dividends that you receive as you allow yourself to awaken into greater awareness.

The fastest way to freedom [**(I)**] is to feel your feelings.

Robert Holden

Look upon awareness as one of the greatest gifts available to us as human beings. It is freely given. We do not have to buy it. We do have to receive it. The dividends paid by your investment in awareness are very considerable indeed.

Just for the heaven of it, stop for a moment to take in five deep slow breaths. As you breathe in, breathe in happiness. As you breathe out, let go of any concerns, fears or preoccupations. Be aware of any feelings as they surface. Breathe in happiness and as you breathe out, let any hurt feelings go. Become aware of your gentleness and your love. Breathe them in with the happiness. Breathe out any last shreds of tightness or tension. With the last two deep breaths, breathe into the loving within you and breathe out any blocks to your loving. Enjoy your freedom!

Don't worry. Be happy. Now!

Holy – or Lonely?

If you were totally on your own, what would be the worst thing that could happen to you? That you might be alone forever? That no one would ever want to be with you ever again? Or would it be, underneath, feeling rejected?

As mentioned earlier, future fears are a product of the imagination directed negatively. The power of the imagination is such that what you fear tends to come upon you. Alternatively, what you anticipate with pleasure can similarly be drawn towards you.

Solitude can be a choice for freedom or for the self-inflicted pain of loneliness. But it can be a time which is used productively for nurturing yourself and getting in touch once again with your values and sense of purpose in life, for gaining greater perspective. You can become more aware of the loving you have for yourself and others and how you might fulfil that loving in greater ways in the future. You may just stand back and rediscover the joy of simply being you.

You can replace the *fear of being abandoned* by *treating yourself abundantly to your gentle loving.*

Choosing Freedom – All the Way to Liberation

Many of us mistakenly strive for freedom outside ourselves because we do not have it inside. For example, by either having exceptional financial resources on the one hand, or none whatsoever on the other hand, we can *seem* to have freedom from financial responsibility (O). When we get apparent freedom (O), all we have done is controlled something – we have not really freed (I) ourselves.

The way we learn peace is by confronting the fears in our own minds and consciousness. We do not confront them in the usual sense. We hold steady within ourselves and simply reconnect deeply with our inner power of loving. The fears move aside, and peace and calm appear, often described as the 'peace that passes understanding'.

That which in the past has seemed to control you now becomes a springboard to your freedom. In a free state of mind, you are able to accept that you really do not know what will happen from moment to moment. You can respond spontaneously to whatever life presents to you, not by exercising control as a way of protecting yourself, but by listening to the inner wisdom of your heart for clear direction.

So, for example, if a close relative or your employer demands something from you that you feel unable to fulfil, you respond from the clarity of your heart with the truth as you experience it and out of caring for yourself and relevant others. You do not have to try and control anyone else. You can make clear choices of freedom for yourself and exercise them accordingly.

In this way, you can replace the *fear of losing control* with the *freedom of living spontaneously*, with your **Possible Dream** as a guiding light.

Grieving the Past

That which you clear up and let go of in the way of commitments, possessions and other attachments in the world **(O)** has a corresponding component of associations, memories and sentiment **(I)**. It is more than natural, it is positively healthy to grieve the past.

However good your experiences were in the past, they really can be replaced by something even better now, your **Possible Dream**. Your unhappy past experiences are best flushed out because those that linger have a way of repeating themselves in the future. It is as though the suffering gets repeated until we learn the lesson that it is designed to give us. The lesson is always one of loving. Suffering is experienced as the result of a lack of loving ourselves in some capacity.

Rather like the emotion of shame explored earlier, grief is an intensely personal emotion that cannot be communicated verbally. The expression of grief is greatly assisted by the loving presence of another person, real or imaginary, who, as it were, is simply there for us as we reach into the source of our pain. It is our loving *touch*, physically or emotionally, that communicates volumes of loving to the one in grief and enables a healing **(I) + (O)** to take place.

The act of grieving your past then is an extraordinary opportunity to awaken into more of your loving, freedom and joy. If grieving does not come naturally to you, it may be that in your family or culture, the experience and expression of deep feeling were not permitted and became frightening for you. But the depth to which you allow yourself to feel your pain is matched by the height to which you can also experience your joy.

Give yourself encouragement with the affirmation:

It is safe for me to feel deeply.

Allow yourself to feel your feelings. Give yourself that freedom. Give yourself that experience because it is not just for yourself that you can develop this capacity. Gaining our freedom is never a selfish pursuit. The freedom we give to ourselves we can also give to others. In fact, we can step into much greater service to those we love, and those we have yet to love, by allowing others the experience and expression of their grief through our heartfelt empathy.

Grief is an important turning-point (I) of expansion into SuperYou, into the world of loving we share with others, not the illusion of separation and distance, which is our suffering.

Forgive yourself for any judgements that you may have made, consciously or unconsciously, that you are separate. In your moments of sadness, extend to yourself your kindness and compassion and allow your new inner connection to awaken you to more of the loving, freedom and joy that await you now, that are part of who you truly are.

Freedom – It's as Easy as ABC

If you had real freedom, could you *live* with it? It's as easy as ABC – and DEF:

A   Attitude
B   Boundaries

C   Commitment
D   Discipline
E   Enthusiasm
F   Fun

Attitude

A positive attitude is much more than positive thoughts alone. 'Attitude' here means the direction or focus you hold for yourself. If you want freedom, use freedom as your focus, whatever that means for you. Hold the images of freedom in your consciousness: physically, mentally, emotionally, spiritually, financially, sexually. When you experience lesser qualities, choose in the moment to refocus (I) on that freedom. It can be as simple as breathing in and breathing out.

Boundaries

Know yourself. Be true to yourself. Know when to say 'No.' It is not a mark against you to admit that you have limitations. After all, none of us can be all things to all people. When you cut away the obligations that do not fit for you, you are freer to honour more fully the steps (I) + (O) you need to take to realize your **Dream**.

If you were designing a building, for example, you might find it extremely difficult if you did not have any parameters of cost, terrain, local requirements, dimensions within which to be creative. Knowing what you want sometimes becomes apparent as you identify what you do not want. Have the courage of your convictions then to cut away that which imposes an unnecessary restriction on your freedom for fulfilment.

Commitment

Live, breathe, feel the joy of your **Dream** into its realization. Let the thoughts that you entertain and the actions that you take be in alignment with your purpose of ever-increasing joy. Through giving yourself fully to your vision in all of its dimensions, you will discover your freedom.

Discipline

For many of us, the idea of discipline is another reason for rebellion. This is probably because we were taught more from the *Law of Control*, than from the *Grace of Intention*, as described in the last chapter. Discipline might have meant falling in line with what others wanted, even when it might have violated your integrity in some way.

The earlier meaning of discipline was that of education and training. It is this sense that applies to freedom. The literal meaning of 'education' is drawing forth from within what is already present, such as your wisdom. 'Training' is putting that inner knowing, the wisdom, into practice.

Your discipline is putting into practice the qualities of freedom and what they mean for you, as you begin to realize the magnificent joy of your **Dream**.

Enthusiasm

Enthusiasm is a quality of boundless energy and possibility. No obstacle is too great. It is a supreme inner quality that is infectious, inspiring and will attract to you the important elements of your **Dream**. If you find at any time that your energy is flagging, you can tap into your enthusiasm for your vision.

Even when you may be opposed, you will know deeply within yourself: *Yes, this* is *possible. Yes, I know there* is *a way this can happen.* Enthusiasm speaks volumes without a word ever being expressed. It comes from the heart of your convictions.

Fun

Whoever said freedom has to be boring and dull? Quite the reverse. Fun is that childlike quality that is willing to entertain what the adult world has condemned as unworkable. It is the outer expression of the inner bubble of joy that cannot help but challenge what has been accepted as the norm, the one and only right way to accomplish a result. Silly? Perhaps. Chaotic? Maybe. Do-able? Absolutely. Watch me!

Freedom ABC

Your Comprehensive Training Programme

Does the idea of a training programme imply for you something rough, tough and rigorous? Getting up at some ungodly hour and undergoing considerable stress, strain and hardship as you attempt to fulfil almost impossible tasks? The regimen of beating yourself up harder so you can be better is definitely not a part of the **Possible Dream**.

Life for many of us is at times quite hard enough already, so why would we want to inflict even more distress upon ourselves? *This* training programme is one of great gentleness and joy, ease, peace and harmony because it is with these qualities that you can most effectively fulfil the vision of who you may become.

In most healthy babies, you see radiant qualities of loving and even joy. There are times now when we need the same tenderness, acceptance, compassion and kindness as we did as a baby growing up. Right now, we can learn to become a better 'parent' to the vulnerable and childlike aspect of our nature. In order to do this effectively, we need to be willing to let go of our limitations from the past and creatively find new ways of self-care that fit for today. Let's go back to our ABC in greater detail.

Attitude

Your Miracle of Upliftment

GOING HOME TO THE HEART OF YOUR LOVING

I am waking up to the freedom of my inner joy.

Potentially, we always have a choice of focus, a choice of where we place our attention, a choice of attitude. Attitude can be seen as the direction in which we lean or move: positively forwards into what we want more of or negatively backwards into the relative lack and limitation of the past. We can lift above the concerns and issues of our daily lives and, with this *altitude*, glimpse the larger picture of our life and the opportunities it holds for us.

In this guided visualization, you have the opportunity to glimpse your road ahead and the crossroads that leads up to it. Where would you go now to experience your loving in the greatest way possible? To the mountains? To the coast? To a warm climate or somewhere cool and invigorating? On an adventure or somewhere quiet and tranquil?

Take in a few deep breaths and allow yourself to become relaxed, receptive and peaceful inside. As before, you may wish to pre-record this visualization, have someone else read it through slowly for you or allow the images to come forward as you read each section. Closing your eyes periodically will assist you to tune inwardly to the images and the information they have for you.

As you relax, feel the sense of anticipation and pleasure ... as you prepare yourself ... you begin to experience an awakening to your freedom ... the freedom as you expand more fully into your loving ...

Envisage yourself lifting above your present location, wherever it is you happen to be ... You might imagine yourself on a magic carpet, in a helicopter, a balloon or any other form of transportation that can take you to a higher viewing-point from which you can travel to your destination ... Let any issues or concerns that may be preoccupying you fade in the distance way below you ...

At this height, all is very peaceful ... The busyness and distractions of your everyday life have faded into insignificance ... You become aware of an all-pervading gentle calmness ... free from disturbance ... and a fine sense of attunement with the heart of who you are ... a knowing that all is right with your world ...

A feeling of your beauty and serenity begins to fill every cell of your body with a new vibrancy ... With increasing joy and delight ... you experience yourself being carried effortlessly forward ... as if you were floating higher and higher in your divine transportation ...

As you glance below you, you can just see in the far distance the road along which you have travelled in your life so far ... What do you notice about that road ...? What are the turns along which it has taken you ...? Were there rough patches ... and uphill struggles ... times when the going was smooth and easy ... with beautiful scenery along the way ...? You now notice a crossroads beneath you ... and the choice of directions you can make ...

One choice is to go back along the route you have just come ... It is at least familiar ... You may recognize the turns ... and know how to negotiate yourself around them ... So the old route is apparently safe ... one over which you might have some control ... but as you look at it more ... it lacks appeal for you ...

You notice some other roads leading off in different directions ... and a signpost in the middle of the crossroads ... as you focus your attention, you notice one route indicated 'Joy, Freedom, Happiness' ... standing out from the others ... Could this road be your life as it is now becoming? ...

Along the path of Joy ... Freedom ... Happiness ... you notice points of light ... like street lighting ... that make this route stand out more brightly than the others ... that make it appear the most welcoming and attractive to you ...

You bring your transportation down to meet this path ... and begin to travel along just above the surface ... It is unfamiliar ... but it is also fun ... Notice the changing scenery ... nothing stays the same for very long ... Slightly lifted above the surface of the road ... you notice the rough patches lit up as you come to them ... and lift a little higher above them ...

Along this path ... you experience a certain buoyancy ... a quality quite different from anything you have previously experienced ... the extra light enables you to lift above the rough patches before you stumble into them

... With this extra clarity and light ... you are also aware of more beauty around you than ever before ...

Your path now takes you up an incline ... and across it right at the top you notice a brightly coloured banner stretching out ... waving a greeting to you ...

Celebrate Yourself!

Celebrate your Freedom!

As you approach it ... you can hear music ... it is the most enriching ... uplifting ... joyous sound you have ever heard ... As you pass beyond the banner ... you are welcomed by the warm faces of many friends who greet and embrace you with their loving ... They rejoice with you as they celebrate your love ... as they recognize the gifts of love that you are ...

You listen to their words of encouragement as they affirm your new freedom ... One special person comes forward extending a gift to you ... to celebrate your life ... What is this gift ...? What does it mean for you ...?

Ecstasy would be a poor word to describe the fullness in your heart now ... You have stepped forward into the expanse of the loving within you ... your world is celebrating your arrival ... you recognize the home that is your heart ... your heart which is always profoundly connected to the best that there is available to you ... to give ... and to receive ...

In the magnificence of your loving ... you experience the inner joy of simply being who you are ... In this moment you know deeply within you that all your needs are being provided for ... whatever they are ... You realize that the path you have chosen is a path of goodness ... and yes ... it feels different to travel with such an abundance *of love ... yet you know that this is the right and only path for you to travel ...*

Each step is perfectly protected and guided by each light along the way ... Each stop is perfectly celebrated with an affirmation of your loving support ... The choice you are making for greater loving is being witnessed and echoed in every way by the world around you ...

The freedom that you are ... the courage you now demonstrate ... you find lights a touch paper for others around you ... they now receive the encouragement they need to live more fully from the heart ... As you realize this ... the joy in your heart expands ... This joy increases as it serves to awaken many others ... seen and unseen ... known and unknown ... The feeling of gratitude for this joy now fills every cell of your body ... healing and releasing any past misperceptions ... misunderstandings ... hurt feelings ... or sadness...

You experience a radiant peace ... quite unlike any you have had before ... In this peace is a stillness ... a pure relaxation of trusting ... of knowing that you are love ... you are loved ... and cared for ...

Keeping the qualities of freedom ... joy ... happiness ... peace ... in your consciousness ... now bring your attention back to this present moment ... and very gradually ... allow yourself to refocus on your immediate world around you ... knowing as you do so that you have a new way of viewing it ... and a new way of viewing yourself within it ...

To complete this exercise, draw the gift that you were given. How does it reflect to you your inner joy? Write down its meaning for you.

For example:

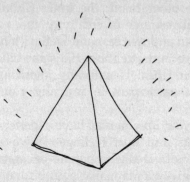

The symbol is a crystal pyramid. It reflects to me the clarity of my intention and my knowing that I can experience and express my inner joy.

Boundaries

Claiming your Inner Joy

I am freely experiencing and expressing my inner joy.

In *Superlove*, one of my previous books, the idea of the Inner Child was fully explored and discussed. To summarize for the purpose of the exercise that follows, the Inner Child is the emotional side of your nature that is akin to who you were around the ages of four to seven. Whatever our age, we retain a childlike nature which, when out of balance, expresses the childish behaviour of moods, tempers, sulkiness, withdrawal, stubbornness, fear, upset, tearfulness and so on.

On the other hand, the Inner Child is also a wonderful resource of creativity, fun, energy and enthusiasm and will respond well with responsible loving care and attention, the same as any child. Your Inner Child is naturally joyful and a very important participant in realizing your **Possible Dream**.

In growing up you may have experienced disappointments and hurt feelings. However diligent and well-motivated your parents or caretakers, they were not given a manual at your birth on how best to educate *you* to live effectively in the world. The Inner Child tends to retain a memory of these events from long ago and then project them onto present experiences.

As you prepare to evolve into your **Possible Dream**, you will be developing a much greater partnership with your Inner Child as the most loving parent you could ever be. You are going to be educating your Inner Child into co-operating more fully with you, and you will find that he or she will respond marvellously with much more energy, enthusiasm and vitality.

This next exercise is a programme for self-care which you can sustain over a 30-day period in order to create better habits of life-support. Through this daily commitment to self-care, your Inner Child will grow to trust you more and therefore co-operate better with you as you establish the clear boundaries of loving attention that honour your needs. What is more, as you learn to give yourself better care, your Inner Child will spontaneously reward you with wisdom, insight and fun.

You will need a notebook, preferably loose-leaf

so that you can insert pages as you wish. Set a starting date for your self-care programme. Count off 30 days to its completion. Write these dates down.

The theme you will be affirming to yourself throughout this period is:

I am taking very good care of myself.

This is the clear intention you will be putting into action as a loving parent to your Inner Child.

You will find it helpful to list under the following headings some of the actions you will take to nurture yourself:

- Physically
- Emotionally
- Mentally
- Spiritually
- Financially
- Sexually
- Treats and Rewards
  Many of us have been 'educated' by punishment for failure, rather than reward for success. You will find that reward for success is much more nurturing, effective and energy-producing. More fun too.
- Supporters
  Make your list of supporters, the friends you can call on during this time. They do not need to know that you are treating yourself to this programme, but they will be people you feel safe with, enjoy talking to or just being with and will therefore be nurturing to you.

Here are some examples:

- Physically
  massages
  warm bath in the evening before bed
  a healthy balanced diet
  walks

- Emotionally
  open, clear communications with friends
  listening to uplifting music
  healing sessions with my counsellor
  relaxation exercises after work

- Mentally
  affirmations to nurture positive thinking
  crossword puzzles
  freeform writing
  clear out any 'dead wood' in my life

- Spiritually
  daily meditation
  give encouragement to others in need
  forgive myself if I get out of balance with self-
  judgements
  record my gratitude for all I have

- Financially
  balance my cheque book
  ask for the pay rise
  set aside some money for treats
  send a donation to my favourite charity

- Sexually
  forgive myself for judging my past sexual behaviour
  tell my partner what I like
  give myself permission to feel passion
  dress to express my sexuality

- Treats and Rewards
  ice cream
  movies
  visit my favourite horse
  go to the beach

For each day of your programme, you will be taking a page and heading it with the date. You might like to choose a different nurturing affirmation for yourself each day as it comes.

What you will *not* be doing is setting yourself an impossibly long list of nurturing 'Things to Do' for the day, which you end up not doing and then feeling bad about. Instead, you will be writing down at the *end of the day* what you have actually done. You will feel better about having accomplished a number of seemingly small nurturing actions which do not take a lot of time than, say, spending half a day soaking in a warm bath. As you establish a loving connection with your Inner Child, he or she will let you know what is most loving for you and when. Intuition, spontaneity and joy will be features of the rapport you have with your Inner Child.

Making conscious choices for the parameters or boundaries that support you will include staying out of situations or away from people that are unnecessarily disturbing or upsetting. Your choices are not *against* anyone else. They are lovingly standing up *for* you. Your boundaries will enable you to say 'Yes' to that expansion now, and 'No' to limitations of the past.

If you have any difficulty thinking about what you might do to take better care of yourself, you might like to refer to some of the exercises in *Superlife* and *Superlove*, all of which are designed to be life-enhancing.

To summarize, the daily page for your self-nurturing programme will be headed with the date and the affirmation:

I am taking very good care of myself.

You might in addition like to choose an affirmation for that particular day. Before you begin your day, glance through your list of nurturing actions to remind yourself of some of the possibilities available to you. You may of course add to this list throughout the programme as new ideas come to mind. In fact, hopefully you will expand into much greater self-care over the 30-day period as you make this a feature and priority in your life.

At the end of each day, make a list of the actions you took and take care to remember each loving accomplishment as you honour your commitment.

Commitment

Be Devoted and Dedicated to your Dream

I am receiving the freedom of my inner joy.

Many of us find it relatively easy to commit our lives to people or projects outside ourselves – to our children, spouse, partner, friends in need; or to our work, social activity or community. However, few of us find it easy to be so generous in giving to ourselves. Yet, paradoxically, it is only when we truly give to ourselves first that we can give our best to those people we love and the projects we value.

In the light of your self-care programme:

- What else do you need to do to connect more fully to your inner joy?
- Who or what from outside **(O)** would stand in the way of your inner joy?
- What does that person or event **(O)** reflect to you about yourself **(I)**?
- How will you exercise freedom in that relationship or situation in order to experience and express more of your inner joy?
- When will you do that?

For example:

- What else do you need to do to connect more fully to your inner joy?

Renegotiate the agreements I have with one friend, to establish more loving boundaries and open up more loving communications between us.

- Who or what from outside **(O)** would stand in the way of your inner joy?

    No one and nothing really – unless I made someone or something else an excuse for not experiencing my inner joy. I could make continuing a game of pretending to be in control of life around me more important than being true to myself and my **Possible Dream**.

- What does that person or event **(O)** reflect to you about yourself **(I)**?

    If I allow anyone or anything to stand in the way of what is really important to me, it reflects to me a lack of courage and loving and a need to nurture more of my loving.

- How will you exercise freedom in that relation- ship or situation in order to experience and express more of your inner joy?

    I will take time and if necessary ask for assistance to get clearer about my motivation and the intention in my heart. When I get clearer about my intention and how to fulfil it, I shall communicate my awareness to the people concerned.

- When will you do that?

    Later on today.

- When you are connected to your inner joy you will be able to exercise real freedom **(I)** in your life. Any time you lose the connection, you know you have gone 'off track'. Maintaining the connection will enable you to realize your **Possible Dream** more effectively. That is your commitment: committing to the inner connection **(I)**. It is up to you to keep warmth in your heart and the passion for your **Dream**!

Discipline

Be Here Now

I am gratefully learning how to exercise freedom with joy.

How did you react at school when someone was about to impose discipline on you? There is something about strict discipline that can bring out the naughtiest rebel in us. Have you ever tried to suppress giggles in a serious environment, such as during a church service? The more you try to control yourself, the more you seem to lose it.

Free-spirited children are often inconvenient in the controlled, sober adult world of appropriate behaviour. Yet it is a sad waste to always quash the exuberance of raw childlike energy. It would be better to accept that energy with love and give it clear, strong, loving direction. Similarly, you need to accept with gratitude your own life energy and give it clear loving direction towards realizing your **Possible Dream**.

The following exercise can be applied to any circumstance that seems to be limiting your freedom. This is a paper and pencil exercise which will, with repetition, reveal to you how you can achieve your freedom. Treat it lightly. It is primarily an exercise in awareness. You need only take action when it is clear for you to do so. You will be working through the following sequence:

- awareness
- choice
- sacrifice
- forgiveness
- freedom

Complete the following statements:

- I am aware that ...
- My choice is to ...
- I am willing to sacrifice (I) or (O) ...
- I forgive myself for feeling afraid that ...
- I am now free to ...

When you come to 'sacrifice', think about letting go first of all of attitudes (I) or patterns of thinking and behaviour that are less than life-enhancing or life-supporting.
For example:

- I am aware that my friendship with Jan is out of balance and causing me to feel unhappy.
- My choice is to accept that her way of looking at life is very different from mine and that essentially our views are incompatible.

- I am willing to sacrifice the pattern in me that demands that people I love have to see everything my way.
- I forgive myself for feeling afraid that if I am true to myself I shall be abandoned by the ones I love.
- I am now free to be truer to myself and share my joy with those I can be close to.

The idea that discipline leads to freedom may be new to you. But it works. Limiting yourself to what really works for you is not a statement of lack and loss. The reverse. The wise expenditure of your energy – financial, physical, mental, emotional, spiritual and sexual – will enable you to experience the grace of abundance. There is absolutely no shortage of anything you really need, and even want, when you are claiming authority over your life, living in freedom and joy.

Enthusiasm

Expand your Energy

My joy is abundant and freely accessible.

The original meaning of *enthusiasm* is literally 'being possessed by divine energy'. If you have difficulty with the phrase 'divine energy', think of it as being 'superloving'. What if divine energy were in and around every aspect of our lives, sustaining all life in and around us? What if aspects of that divine energy were in all the rocks, plants, flowers, animals and ourselves? What if through the intimate connection to our own divine nature we could tap into and access a tremendous network of spiritual power that is constantly available to us? Then perhaps what we ask for, we could receive, because there would be absolutely no shortage, other than in our thinking.

The doubter in you may now respond with all kinds of arguments as to why this wouldn't work. After all, you might say, there is a lot of lack and limitation around. Undeniably so. You are free, of course, to argue for your limitations, but this will not lead you towards greater joy.

Recall a time when you experienced most enthusiasm. It might have been many years ago, when as a child you were about to go on holiday or be taken for a treat. Or it could have been when you were about to conclude a deal and you absolutely *knew* it was going to turn out right. Or possibly waking up to bright sunshine on a winter weekend filled with inspiration for your day, doing something you really want to do.

With enthusiasm comes a timelessness or an abundance of time. With enthusiasm you find pleasure in life's simplicity; all your needs are more than fulfilled. With enthusiasm, alone or with others, you enjoy a delightfully happy communion with life.

Imagine there were a radio station you could turn to: Enthusiasm FM, 101.5 on your radio dial. Yes, Enthusiasm is a matter of attunement! It is inexhaustible, 24 hours a day, 365 days a year, serving the community. What is more, you can choose

166

your own programmes. Music requests – no problem. Inspiring stories from the world at large. Stories of extraordinary human accomplishment. Yes, even miracles. If your reception is not so clear, you can adjust your dial – or maybe move your antennae to a better position of receptivity. The signal is constantly going out – all you have to do is find it. Tune in and enjoy!

Plugged in now as you are to Enthusiasm FM, you can write out your requests. What is your **Possible Dream**? What is it deep down you really want? Or what is it that might lead you to your **Dream**? Do not be concerned if you still do not have the magnitude of your **Dream** in all of its dimensions right now. Your **Dream** may just be a mystery, yet to be fully revealed to you.

You are going to be writing a request to the General Operations Director of Radio Station Enthusiasm FM. You can address him or her as GOD for short. Remember, when you are tuned in clearly, ask and you will receive. One thing to remember about GOD is that you never quite know when your request is going to come over the airwaves – so you must keep listening for the signals.

Take a clean sheet of paper now and start:

Dear GOD ...

For example:

Dear GOD,
I would really like a nice holiday. I have been working quite intensively for some time now and I

would like a break – in the sunshine somewhere where I can meet lovely people, who are open, enthusiastic and very friendly. You know what it is about being on holiday: you don't have to do anything and yet everything you do is fun and interesting. When it stops being fun and interesting, you just stop doing it and do something else. When you want to sleep, you can sleep. If you want to stay up late watching a good movie, you can do that.

Then I would like a few really good books to read. A juicy novel perhaps. An insightful spiritual sort of book and maybe a surprise book I just happen to see on an airport bookshelf. And I would like just a few new clothes to take with me on holiday. Pretty bright colours. I cannot think of anywhere special to go. Do you have any good ideas for me?

With love,

Anne

Once you have written out your request to GOD, you may wish to put it into an envelope and mail it. The post office may have already had to handle GOD's mail for all you know. Or you could put it to one side to review later. Or you could even let it go to GOD by burning it.

As in the example above, you may come up with a question or two for GOD. Here is an opportunity to receive a reply from GOD – GOD always answers, if not immediately. You do have to listen quite carefully and be reasonably open and loving. Emotional upset such as anger, irritation and frustration with GOD tends to close down the lines of communication.

If this seems an unusual exercise for you to do, experiment with it and simply explore how it feels for you. Perhaps the greatest risk is that you might feel silly. The reward, however, may pleasantly surprise you.

For example:

Dear Anne,

Where to go? I have given you a lot of places to choose from – I admit it could be difficult deciding which of them to go to.

I think you might like Hawaii. How does that sound for you? Just a suggestion. Think about it for a while.

With love,

GOD

Now, if GOD came up with an answer like that for you, your first reaction might be: 'Impossible. Too far away. Couldn't possibly afford it.' Watch your inclination towards lack and limitation if that shows up because you never really know what might be right around the next corner. Remember: keep tuned in to Enthusiasm FM, 101.5 on your radio dial.

So make those requests! You have nothing to lose but your limitations!

Fun

Just for the Heaven of It!

I am giving from the freedom of my joy.

Of all the fun-ny things we get up to, sex has to be one of the funniest. Imagine arriving from another planet and observing earthly humans doing sexual activities and seeming to enjoy, yes enjoy, them. The casual observer would notice that sex seems to involve a lot of pursuit and angst, sometimes culminating in marital agreements, which (if statistics are to be believed) have a 50/50 chance of 'success'. Are these humans quite crazy, or what? How on earth do they manage to have any fun when they are constantly attempting to measure up to expectations, standards **(O)** and appearances they have adopted from others? They are very funny, only most of the time they do not seem to realize it.

Fear, mentioned a few times already, has to be the fun-killer of all time. What if fun or fear is really a choice, totally in your hands, all of the time? What fear? Fear of history repeating itself, of making the same mistakes again? Don't look back into your history and re-create it in your mind.

Come into the present moment now, see your situation with fresh eyes and bring the spontaneity of your creative response to produce a new, more rewarding experience. Let go of your past and any difficulties it may have held for you. Appreciate whatever is immediately in front of you, with joy **(I)** and fun **(O)**. Wake up to more fun in your life! Yes, even to the sex in your life.

In this exercise, you will discover that simply who you are is enough. You do not have to live up to anything outside yourself. Truly being who you are is its own reward because there is an absence of pressure and a natural flow of your innate talents.

Turn back to the exercise 'What Are You Hiding?' *(page 11)* If you have not already done it, this exercise will once again get you in touch with some of the qualities and assets you perhaps do not express and share as fully as you could. So do it now. As you reconnect with those qualities, those blessings you already are, allow yourself to feel joy awakening more fully within you.

This next exercise is one you will be practising over the next 24 hours. It is in the form of a dare. Dare to be different! Express your qualities of loving. Expand your possibilities for sharing who you are. Come into the freedom of your joy. Do not be concerned about how, or whether, others will receive your love, or not. What you will be doing is exploring and experimenting with sharing your loving in ways which are the most fun for you.

You might like to make a few notes before you set off. Answer the following questions and allow whatever answers pop into mind to be written down. No censorship! The one where you think 'I couldn't *possibly* do *that*!' could be the most rewarding.

- How did you enjoy sharing your loving as a child?
- How could you find a similar way to share your loving now?

- What have you always wanted to contribute, but have never quite had the courage to do so?
- With whom would you most like to share your loving?
- With whom would you least like to share your loving?
- How could you be truly daring?
- What would be the most courageous action you could take in the next 24 hours?
- How could you make the next 24 hours the most fun you have ever had?
- How will you be giving from the freedom of your joy?

If you did not come up with answers to any of the questions above, do not be concerned. Keep your mind open and you may find yourself 'living' your answers as you spontaneously respond to whatever the moment presents to you.

Bear in mind the following guidelines for this exercise:

> Take care of yourself,
> so you can help take care of others.
>
> Do not hurt yourself,
> and do not hurt others.
>
> Use everything that shows up
> for the greatest good of yourself and others.

What is the time now? Your exercise has now begun! Make a note for exactly this time tomorrow to record what you did and how you expanded your experience of fulfilment.

The doubter in you may come up with: 'So what if I have the worst day of my life?' It really does not have to be that way. This is not an exercise in passing or failing. Remember how in hindsight, disasters can become very humorous? However bad things may seem to get, the SuperYou in you can always make a choice for freedom and joy.

If you know you could have 'done better', wonderful! Learn from your last experience. Select another 24 hours and try for an improvement. As mentioned before, always, in all ways, you are a winner. *How* and *what* you win is your choice and your choice alone.

ABC Free! A Summary

To summarize, your comprehensive training programme for exercising freedom will progress through the ABC stages below. You will find that this programme will give you the strengths you need to realize your **Possible Dream**.

A – Attitude
I am waking up to the freedom of my inner joy.
B – Boundaries
I am freely experiencing and expressing my inner joy.
C – Commitment
I am receiving the freedom of my inner joy.
D – Discipline
I am gratefully learning how to exercise freedom with joy.
E – Enthusiasm
My joy is abundant and free.

F – Fun
I am giving from the freedom of my joy.

Chapter 4: Theme Exercises

Exercising Freedom

Do you really have all the joy now you could ever want? Or do you still have a few dusty corners of doubt that could be swept out to make more space for joy to fill them? The theme exercises for exercising freedom are all to do with nurturing the joy in you. Through your joy you will discover the freedom with which to realize your **Dream**.

The following mini-exercises on joy will assist you in reconnecting inwardly to the source of energy you will need for fulfilling your **Dream**.

1. *Re-see-ving*
   Look again with fresh eyes at any circumstance that may be disturbing to you (I) or (O). Look on the light side. Start to look for the blessings in disguise. They are there! The next time you are aware of being disconnected from your joy, repeat and spontaneously complete the following:
   If this feeling of ... were a blessing in disguise, I would be receiving ...

2. *Any feeling of emotional doubt is like a small cloud that is temporarily covering up a quality that is about to emerge. What if you were to pass through the doubt, what might you find? Deep down, you know very well.*
   What if any negative emotion you experience is simply a doubt cloud, laden with cleansing moisture to release the joy of the inner SuperYou? The darkness of doubt is simply the light travelling in disguise.

*Take a few minutes now to imagine yourself floating
through a mist of the most pure cleansing light. Close your
eyes. Allow yourself to feel each tiny drop of fresh clear
water touch your skin, to share its sweet music and lift
your spirits to new heights. Do this exercise in refreshment
three times a day for the next seven days – and notice how
much better you feel!*

3. *Wake up to your joy!*
   *Have you ever gone to sleep with a problem on your mind
   and woken up with the solution? Imagine what might
   happen if you went to sleep with a solution on your mind?
   Before you go to sleep tonight, listen to some uplifting
   music, contemplate an object of beauty, read an inspiring
   sentence or two – awaken yourself to more of your beauty
   (I). As you go to sleep, repeat gently to yourself the word
   'joy', over and over. Sing it in your mind. Giggle it. Send
   yourself to sleep, bathed in divine humour. And wake up to
   more of your joy!*

4. *See yourself as a tree ...*
   *Choose a favourite tree. What is it? A sturdy oak? A wispy
   poplar? An evergreen fir, all covered with sticky cones? A
   palm tree, swept in tropical breezes? Feel yourself firmly
   planted in the earth, held in cozily by just enough soil and
   moisture. Envisage the joy of this moisture coming up
   through your roots, filling up all your cells as it breaks
   through the surface of the ground and into your trunk.
   Listen as your life juices surrender upwards into the celebration of your branches and twigs, and the healing green of
   your leaves or needles.*
   *Spend a day, or half a day, or what about the next hour, cele-
   brating the free abundance of your tree of joy!*

5. *I deserve more joy ...*
   *The negativity which sometimes traps us into all kinds of
   lack and limitation will often cause us to place obstacles in*

175

our way. If so far in these exercises you have not yet become totally ridiculous (and who is the judge of that?), here is your opportunity to excel yourself with a little divine madness.

Complete the following as ridiculously, and as often, as possible, particularly at times such as standing in line at the post office, driving in heavy traffic, being awoken at an ungodly hour by the noisy neighbours, etc ...

I deserve more joy because ...

6. Joy for me is ...
   Take a sheet of paper and in large letters write across the middle:

$$J \quad O \quad Y$$

Make a mind-map out of the big 'O' by drawing 10 lines and writing on each one a different aspect of what joy is for you. If you get stuck, be silly. In fact, that is an important principle you can apply any time you may be feeling stuck, emotionally or otherwise. No amount of negativity is really worth taking too seriously.

For example:

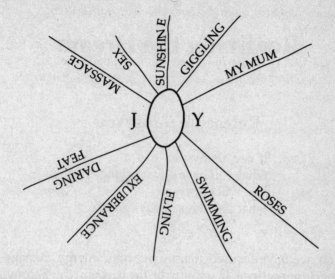

5

Realizing the Dream

Releasing SuperYou

If you always do
what you have always done –
You will always get
what you have always gotten.
Anon

So far we have focused mainly on inner energy management (**Innergetics©**). In order to be the best you can become,
you need to express the inherent goodness that you are in
the outer world. This reality is not hard-nosed as such. Like
the quality of inner power described earlier, your **Dream**
will become real through a light, soft-edged touch, with
energy and enthusiasm, clarity and persistence as you
expand your active involvement in life.

It may not be true to say that we are born with an entirely
blank canvas on which to paint our lives. When we look at
the outer world (**O**), we are obviously not all born equal.
And even children within the same family environment
demonstrate disparate personalities. What if we were born
with unique predispositions to *attract* certain events and
experiences in life?

When we focus on our *inner* world (**I**), there we meet true
equality. Each of us potentially has equal access to an

infinite source of loving. Not one of us is excluded. Deep within you, you are already the best you can become. Realizing your **Dream** is to translate your innate inner perfection into an everyday reality.

Waking Up to your Greater Reality

Lay not up for yourselves treasures upon earth, where moth and rust doth corrupt, and where thieves break through and steal:

But lay up for yourselves treasures in heaven, where neither moth nor rust doth corrupt, and where thieves do not break through nor steal:

For where your treasure is, there will your heart be also.

The light of the body is the eye: if therefore thine eye be single, thy whole body shall be full of light.

... take no thought, saying, What shall we eat? or, What shall we drink? or, Wherewithal shall we be clothed?

... for your heavenly Father knoweth that ye have need of all these things.

But seek ye first the kingdom of God, and his right-eousness; and all these things shall be added unto you.

Matthew 6:19–22, 25, 32, 33

You may be one of many who are currently disenchanted with the models of leadership presented in the world. Few leaders in government, health, education, the Church, law and order or commerce seem to be offering us guidance to attain a secure, pleasurable and fulfilling life. The reality is that no one else, however seemingly influential and wise, can truly direct our life for us as an *external* figure of author-ity. It is time we each now claimed authority over our own lives. Using the tremendous wealth of inner resource which, for the most part, we have not been educated to understand and appreciate to the full, we can enter the greater reality of the **Possible Dream**.

What if, for much of your life so far, you have really been walking around in a daze, doing the best you can under the circumstances and yet somewhat surprised from time to time by unexpected events? What if the natural order of life were actually chaotic, one over which we truly have no control? Contrary to popular belief and expectation, perhaps this chaos is simply a loving framework within which we can learn to co-operate with ease, fun and fulfilment. It is possible to be *in* the world, but not *of* it.

The starting-point for realizing your **Dream**, as already mentioned, is your inner reference point of quiet joy, within which you can entertain the **Dream** in peaceful loving detachment. Here is an exercise to promote your joy.

Claim your Identity as a Loving Person

Anchor your Joy

Inwardly, scan your life so far, in 5-year chunks if you are under 30, and in 10-year chunks if you are over 30, recalling instances, however fleeting and brief, of pure joy. These could be moments when you were helpless with laughter for no reason at all, when a scene in nature struck you with sheer awe, when you were transported by a piece of music or a painting, when you fell in love **(I)** in surrender to the beauty **(O)** you saw in another person, moments of glee when as a child you did something you knew you shouldn't.

These instances might be described as moments of original innocence, when you were captured in the spontaneity of the moment, unencumbered by any limitation. Wouldn't it be great to reconnect with that at any time?

In this exercise you will be 'anchoring' these moments. An 'anchor' is a physiological reference point, a connection between the physical body and an emotional state of mind. For example, a person may scratch the side of his or her head when shy or uncertain. For the most part, such a mannerism is unconscious. However, we can *consciously* use the association of body contact and emotional state to strengthen and enhance the inner connection we would most like to enjoy.

Choose a discreet mannerism which you will recognize as a signal (I) for your joy, but which will not be obvious to anyone else. For example, it might be holding your first two fingers to your thumb, touching your ear or rubbing the tips of the little finger and thumb on your left hand.

Select a minimum of three joyous moments from your past. As you recall each one and the joy it held for you, activate your anchor so that you have a physiological connection with the joy. Reflect for a moment as you do this and allow a simple image to come to mind that similarly connects you to the joy. Draw it in a journal or on a piece of adhesive paper, somewhere that you can refer to it periodically. You may also wish to write the word 'joy' somewhere on or by your symbol and say it inwardly.

For example:

1. Radio Microphone

A programme in which the interviewer and I
enjoyed a lot of fun and laughter.

2. Tennis Racquet

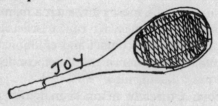

Playing tennis with my Mum when I couldn't play
for collapsing into giggles.

3. Sunrise

Waking up to a new day filled with awe and gratitude for my life.

Once you have anchored your joy, claim your identity as a loving person by spontaneously completing the following statement opening at least five times:

As loving person, I ...

For example:

As a loving person, I choose to focus on the beauty in my life.
I treat myself lightly.
I forgive myself for the mistakes I made in the past.
I make others laugh.
I give myself time to 'zone out' periodically.

When you are really ready to make advances in your life, try completing the statement 50 times! You are already a loving person: you just need to claim it. Lift yourself above the illusion that you might be anything else.

Whenever you need to strengthen the inner connection to your joy, activate your anchor by recalling one of the images and making the physiological connection.

Joy has a way of being infectious. Once you entertain a joyous frame of mind, others around you will awaken to their own. It is best not to let others know what your anchor is, however, or the significance of your symbol. But you could share the technique with them so that they can choose their own anchor, if they wish.

Creating a New Reality
(I) (O)

And I saw a new heaven and a new earth:
for the first heaven and the first earth were passed
away.

Revelation 21:1

What if our *ultimate* purpose in life were to enjoy the freedom to experience many aspects of living? What if, in the
process of gaining our experiences, we were also free to
make mistakes and, more importantly, to learn from them,
through loving ourselves unconditionally? The worst thing
about a mistake is the punishment we level against
ourselves for it. Mistakes may be blessings in disguise. In
hindsight, they are often a source of humour and laughter.

Perhaps the first mistake is one of perception, that
anything you ever do is 'wrong' in the larger picture of your
life. It is an unnecessary judgement. So, forgive it. Instead of
punishing yourself, love yourself enough to learn how you
created, promoted or allowed a result you did not like; if
possible, correct it, forget it and then move on.

Similarly, the ultimate purpose of any *immediate goal*
might be to awaken you more fully to the loving, compassion, wisdom, courage and kindness that you are in your
spiritual heart.

Revealing your Purpose

Learning to Love – Loving to Learn

This is the true joy in life, the being used for a purpose recognized by yourself as a mighty one ... the being a force of nature instead of a feverish selfish little clod of ailments and grievances complaining that the world will not devote itself to making you happy.

George Bernard Shaw

How would you recognize your purpose in life? How might it be useful to you? And how can you discover it?

Have you ever in the past had moments in which you felt you were 'on track', experiencing fulfilment in what you were doing and a sense of your place and belonging in the world? These high points **(I)** from the past will give you clues to your lifelong purpose.

We are often accustomed to looking into the past to find our faults and failings. If only we had done this that or the other differently, we might already be in paradise. Were you ever taught, directly or otherwise, that if you were perfectly 'good' you would be loved by those who matter to you and enjoy a rich and rewarding life? Perhaps you have buried your supposed inadequacies, *fearing* that if others were to discover your imperfections, you might be seriously cast down – and out. Yet, as we have seen, were you to recognize and accept your weaknesses as opportunities for learning and growth you could positively enhance your purpose and personal fulfilment.

Your purpose then is the direction in which you can sustain and expand the loving in your life. It will be broad

185

enough in definition to embrace many different forms of expression, depending upon whatever skills you may be using at any time, your career or vocation and the people with whom you are involved.

Purpose has more to do with your evolving *being* **(I)** throughout your lifetime, however, than your specific *doing* **(O)** at any time. It will have a component of loving fulfilment that will be meaningful, possibly only to you. No one else but you can know when you are on target and for this reason, it is sometimes best to treat your purpose as personal and private rather than tell others about it.

To know your purpose is not a matter of life and death. If and when it is important to you to know it, however, you can inwardly ask and when the time is right, it will be revealed to you. This is a case of ask and you will receive, knock and the door will be opened to you.

If you are not ready to believe that you in fact do have a purpose, why not introduce yourself to the possibility? Try some affirmations along the lines of:

It is possible for me to know my purpose.
I can know my purpose.

If you are really keen to know your purpose, you may inadvertently block yourself from receiving it by being over-anxious. In which case, words like the following may work for you:

In perfect timing I shall know clearly my purpose.

I am enjoying the steady process of discovering my purpose.

If your mind is relaxed, receptive and open you might use the following affirmation:

I know my purpose.

In the exercise that follows, you can begin to open your mind to your purpose. This will assist you to see clearly the most effective steps you need to take to realize the **Dream**. When you enjoy *purposeful* effort, you will be working smarter rather than harder to accomplish your aims. The emphasis in your daily experience will one of greater quality, rather than excessive quantity, of application to achieve a stated result. Your time can really work effectively for you.

Finding your Purpose Within

The Transforming Power of Love

Divine Love is the most powerful chemical
in the Universe.
Divine Love dissolves everything
which is not of itself.

In this exercise, by reviewing the lessons of your past experiences you will begin to recognize the trend of your life purpose. These lessons are quite unlike the kind of learning you probably underwent in school or university. For a start, there is no pass or fail. There is only repeating the lesson or experience until you have fully learnt and completed it – and then forgotten that it was ever a lesson at all!

You will receive no outer award, degree certificate, qualification or any other symbol **(O)** of success, but you will experience **(I)** the greater freedom of no inhibiting past memory. This is the greater freedom that will enable you to realize your **Dream**.

As in the previous exercise, you will be reviewing your life so far in 5- or 10-year chunks. This time, you will be recalling instances of unhealed pain or regret. This takes courage, so be very gentle with yourself as you do this. You do not need to dig around for grievances. You will be given just what you are currently equipped to resolve. Do not judge any incident or experience as being apparently too small to be considered.

What if there were a higher purpose to each of these hurts? What might it be? You have a voice of wisdom within you, your Inspirational Self (for a full description, see *Superlove*). In this exercise you will be conducting a dialogue, using pen and paper, with your Inspirational Self to discover the learning concealed in past pain and the loving required to release yourself from it.

Your dialogue may evolve similarly to the example below:

Me   The experience that comes to mind is a
        time when I was going out for a walk with
        Mum. I was about two or three. I cannot
        remember what led up to it but Mum
        closed the front gate, leaving me behind it,
        and waved goodbye. I felt upset that I was
        being abandoned.
Inspirational Self   Do you remember what led
        up to that?
Me   No. Well, I might have been fussing a bit...
IS   Do you know what you might have

	been fussing about?
Me	I could have been having a battle of wills with my mother.
IS	*Could* have?
Me	Yes, was having.
IS	How did that feel for you?
Me	I wanted to get my way so I was feeling pretty determined. I felt as though my mother was being bossy.
IS	What was *your* way?
Me	I am not sure I remember.
IS	If you were to guess?
Me	I was feeling hurt about something at the time.
IS	Can you remember what that was?
Me	I think I had been feeling daydreamy and Mum wanted me to get a move on. I was enjoying my thoughts and she shook me out of them and I felt irritated by that. So I got back at her by being moody. She told me that her intention was to go out for a walk and if I wanted to be left behind, I would find out about that.
IS	That all sounds pretty reasonable. Have you ever had experiences similar to that since then?
Me	Yes.
IS	If I understood right, you have a 'dreamy' part of your nature, which for the most part is valid and important to you. Is that accurate?
Me	Yes.
IS	Good. Then there are times when you need to switch out of being dreamy to co-operate

189

with a different activity being offered by, say, a 'higher' power taking care of you, such as your mother. Is that accurate?

Me   Yes.

IS   Did you ever criticize either that dreamy side of your nature and/or your mother as a result of that early interaction and perhaps misunderstanding?

Me   Yes. By the way, how come you know so much about what goes on with me?

IS   Just say I have some insider information ... Are you ready to be more loving and to forgive yourself for those judgements?

Me   I am. I forgive myself for judging myself. I forgive myself for judging my mother as being authoritarian.

IS   Can you see how those judgements were an attempt to gain some control and take care of your needs as you saw them – and that now in hindsight your caring can be expressed differently?

Me   How do you mean?

IS   Are you ever too strict and authoritarian with yourself?

Me   Sometimes.

IS   Can you see that the criticism you make against *others* sticks to you – and hurts?

Me   Mmm.

IS   So how now can you be more loving?

Me   How about this? I can accept both the daydreamy and authoritarian sides of *my own* nature and, being aware of them, allow each of them to serve me in a greater way, sort of more co-operatively.

IS   Is that it? By the way, what does 'sort of more co-operatively' mean for you?

Me   Along the lines of to everything there is a season, and a time to every purpose – or something like that. I can be responsible for the times when I am dreamy and recognize when it is time to move into another activity. When I am listening inwardly and responding to my inner direction, I never have to be hard on myself – I can flow with my inner guidance.

IS   Or alternatively, abandon *yourself* – but that hurts, which was where we came in, was it not?

Me   To recap: when I remember to listen inwardly for direction and guidance I know full well how I can best be using my time and energy. When I do not listen to myself in this way, it is like abandoning myself as at that gate and feeling cut off from the source of my loving, which I saw as my Mum when I was a toddler. That feels better. Thank you!

IS   Don't mention it.

Conclude this exercise with statements relating to the learning you received. Keep in mind your emerging sense of purpose. Along the following lines:

I learnt that ...
My purpose is ...

I learnt that I can appreciate all sides of my nature.
... I can also appreciate all sides of others' natures.

... I cannot get away with criticizing others without hurting myself.

... there is a value in listening inwardly to my own direction.

... I may be more caring by giving myself the gift of flexibility.

... My purpose is to learn co-operation and enjoy the benefits of greater inner attunement and flexibility.

You may need to explore as few as three past events to discover your higher purpose of learning in life. Allow your purpose to emerge gradually, like pieces in a puzzle coming together, until you know clearly what it is. Should you find yourself getting impatient, it could be that learning patience is a part of your purpose!

If your mind is blank it may be that a period of your life is already complete, healed and peaceful for you. It could also be that you are not yet ready to heal a particular hurt.

Do not be put off by thinking *your* way of doing this exercise might be entirely different, possibly 'wrong'. Trust yourself that only by doing it, you can make discoveries that are valuable for you.

Be Patient –
The Journey May Be Half the Fun!

The exercise of discovering your purpose is a learning process in itself. So be patient. You can keep your eye on the intention of knowing your purpose by affirming, last thing at night and first thing in the morning:

I know my purpose.

All too often, we tend to give up when we do not get what we want at the first attempt. We block ourselves by making our aim an 'issue' or a problem to be solved, rather than keeping with the process of revelation, for as long as it may take, until we arrive.

Imagine you are going on holiday to some remote Caribbean island. There might be several stages to your journey and the latter ones can only be revealed as you come closer to your destination. Had you heard about the final off-beat boat trip before you set off, you might have been discouraged from ever departing in the first place! Yet the funky boat trip could turn out to be the most hilarious part of your whole journey.

Let's try another exercise.

Know your Purpose!

Your purpose is deeply personal. Only you can know the truth of it. Just imagine that even before you were born you entered a contract of tremendous love. Embodied in this contract was an agreement to understand the nature of love in a much greater way and in exchange for this precious gift of understanding you agreed to make a unique contribution of some kind.

You might look at your life and wonder what on earth could be particularly 'unique' about it and your contribution. It has been said that no two snowflakes are alike. So in this vast orchestra of humanity do any of us play precisely the same note – even supposing that we might be playing in accord?

This exercise in revealing your purpose can be done in gentle stages. Once each day for the following seven days, spontaneously complete the statement below without giving it too much thought:

My purpose is ...

For example:
My purpose is to serve others.
... to love God.
... to know God.
... to know that I am divine.
... to expand in the quality of my giving.
... to be happy.
... to enjoy my wealth **(I)** and **(O)**.
... to assist others to be happy.
... to communicate my love.
... to be serene.
... to be at peace.
... to have fun.
... to enjoy the beauty in and around me.

The statements are like pieces of a jigsaw puzzle. Together they will give you your bigger picture. When you are ready to receive it, your purpose will appear and you will easily recognize it.

Thinking too much can often block us from receiving a deeper level of inner awareness, so simply *do* the exercise in loving detachment – and begin to enjoy living your purpose.

Living with Integrity

Being able to enjoy success is the best reason for achieving it.

Translating inner alignment with your purpose into your everyday reality is a matter of keeping your purpose in view and then keeping your eyes focused on that vision. Supposing your vision were two to five years away, as you approached its fulfilment, you would refocus or 'course correct' in order to stay in alignment with your purpose.

PURPOSE
Lifelong

↑

20 YEAR VISION

↑

INTERMEDIATE VISIONS
2-5 years

↑

DAILY FOCUS
Now

Rather like the series of three beacons the Romans used when building a straight road, you will be using the beacons of your purpose and visions to maintain alignment in your daily involvements **(I) + (O)**. Your daily focus will be supporting your vision and your vision will be supporting your purpose.

You've got to think about big things while you're doing small things, so that all the small things go in the right direction.

Alvin Toffler

End Result Visioning

I always wanted to be a somebody, but I should have been more specific.

Lily Tomlin

Now it's time to envision our **Dream** in greater detail – but still remain patient. Many of our major life transitions, such as bereavement, retirement or a radical improvement in any area of attitude, belief and behaviour, generally take two years to be complete. For example, achieving a new body weight is not just a question of a crash diet to lose unwanted inches. Attaining the desired weight is only the beginning. Sustaining the weight, with a strong esteem and a healthy pattern of nutrition, is the more complete vision.

Other projects, such as attaining a career objective, may take three or even five years. As has been said before and is worth repeating, the big mistake to avoid is that of trying to accomplish too much too soon and then giving up in discouragement.

With any objective that seems huge, find a way to break it down into small, manageable and achievable chunks. You will also need to stop frequently, to track your progress and realign yourself with the direction you have set yourself. We shall look more closely at setting time limits before creating the end result vision in the next exercise.

Working with Time on your Side

The closer a goal or objective, the more accurately you will be able to pinpoint the time you need to complete it. For example, you may have a deadline to write a report, a time at which you have to pick up the children from school today or a number of specific tasks to finish during the morning.

Objectives dealing with personal re-education, by which I mean letting go of self-destructive habits or patterns of behaviour, are more difficult to pin down. When we put pressure on ourselves, we may experience the conflict of inner rebellion and ultimate defeat, which can further reinforce the very pattern we are attempting to replace.

As has been said before, a first step is to recognize, accept and appreciate that *any habit* that you are now labelling as less than desirable was once a form of life support for you. Drugs, sex, alcohol, gambling or any other dependency may have given you the means to make life tolerable in some way. So do not underestimate the time required to establish a higher level of choice and creativity to improve your quality (I) of life. For example, suppose you would really like to give up smoking, but right now you have a stronger desire to keep smoking. You may be someone who can only give something up by making the decision to stop today and never let a cigarette be in your hand again. That is certainly an effective way to do it. However, it can also be a shock to the system.

An alternative is to give yourself a minimum of two years to become your own 'smoke free zone'. You may take a year to work on establishing a strong healthy inner vision, researching in a gentle way all the various methods and techniques for giving up smoking, without committing yourself to taking up any one of them.

Similarly, the adjustment to entering so-called 'retirement' from full-time economic activity is best approached as a two-year period of acclimatization. Often, in the first year of retirement, a person can be approached by any number of organizations which recognize an opportunity for volunteer help. It is best to allow a full year of retirement during which to research all the possibilities before making a commitment to those which will provide greatest pleasure and satisfaction, and will be in alignment with your personal purpose.

This idea can also be applied to adopting a healthier pattern of nutrition in which you are enjoying the body weight that feels most comfortable for you and best reflects your esteem.

Prolonged suffering in any area of your life is needless. Not only is it possible, but it is positively desirable to create a normal state of balance, harmony and enjoyment (I) in your life as a whole. So regard any discomfort as one of those wake-up calls to greater self-awareness.

In Chapter 2, Using your Resources, we explored money partly as an issue and partly as a resource. For many of us, money is a highly emotive subject one way or the other because it surfaces some of our deepest concerns for survival itself which may go back to our earliest months or even days of life. When you get clear about what it is you *really* want in life, the area of comfort which is most likely to be challenged is that of your relationship with money. For example, your *dependency* on a good salary and the benefits that go with a managerial job may be the greatest obstacle to your embarking on fulfilling a heartfelt career ambition or vocation.

With career or occupation moves, you may look at a three-year period of preparation and training. So the idea here is not to hand in your notice tomorrow and put your family home and the children's education at risk in the process, but work through to your end result vision, your **Dream**.

As you start creating an end result vision you will be replacing any anxieties associated with survival with the inner qualities of abundance associated with being the best you can become.

Creating your Vision

People are always blaming their circumstances for what they are.
I don't believe in circumstances.
The people who get on in this world are the people who get up and look for the circumstances they want, and, if they can't find them, make them.

George Bernard Shaw

The process of creating an end result vision is very simple. It is visioning for the success that you want, creating your new reality from the inside out **(I) (O)**, *as if it were already accomplished*. The more vivid your vision, the more effective will be the process of achieving the end result. It is wise not to lock your vision into a time schedule. You may have a sense that the results could arrive within a two- to five-year period but it is best not to be rigid about this.

You could apply this exercise to a new body weight programme, replacing any unhealthy dependency with greater self-care, enhancing personal relationships, gaining financial stability or achieving more fulfilment in your occupation — anything you want, in fact!

Very often we are shaken out of a current condition because we are not happy with it and it has become a problem. A good question to ask is: what would your life be like if you did not have this problem? If your life could be as good as it might possibly be, what would that be like for you? What would you be noticing? It is important to bring to mind some clear specific images that you can experience inwardly as dynamically real and vibrantly life-like.

The idea here is that you create inwardly an abundantly clear experience which you will anchor with your joy *(see pages 180–83)* to increase the sense of reality of your vision. The clearer the vision, the clearer will be the means and methods with which you will realize it.

You will be writing a statement that describes your end result vision. Engage all your senses as you begin to imagine it, *as if it had already happened*. Take yourself forward to a date from two to five years from today's date. What will the date be? Write that date down. Go for the very best that you can possibly imagine as you reflect on the following questions:

- How will the situation look?
- How will you look?
- What does your environment look like?
- What do you notice in your field of vision?
- How does your success appear to you?

- What sounds are associated with your vision?
- What do you hear being said to you?
- What do you hear yourself saying to you?

- What do you hear yourself communicating with others?
- How does your success sound to you?

- How do you feel about yourself?
- What positive sensations are you aware of in your body?
- What inner qualities make you feel particularly good?
- How does your success feel for you?

- What special tastes or smells are related to your vision?
- What does your success taste like?
- What does your success smell like?

If you are envisioning a new body weight, you could see yourself buying clothes in a new size, seeing your slimmer body in the mirror, feeling freer, fitter and lighter, seeing the weight shown on the scales, hearing congratulations from your friends, really enjoying the foods that best support your new weight. Write it all down in full.

If you are envisioning financial balance, you can imagine your peace of mind as you receive the bills you can confidently pay, issuing invoices that truly reflect the worth of the work you do, enjoying spending appropriate money for pleasure, watching your savings account steadily increasing, seeing your accounts in balance, feeling that your needs are more than being met. Leave no detail unturned in your written account.

If you are envisioning freedom from your dependency on alcohol, feel the ease with which you can walk past a bar or refuse the offer of a drink, see shelves in your home with books or music in place of bottles of wines and spirits, see yourself comfortable as you are expressing your feelings with your loved ones, hear the new confidence in your voice, experience the pleasure of eating in a new way, feel the peace of your honesty and freedom from guilt and shame, get in touch with the gentle power of your loving in a whole new way. Get all those details down as you fully and comprehensively imagine your successful end result.

The secret to success with this exercise might be:

Know what you *really* want.

Connect **(I)** to your joy.

Go after it **(O)**!

Track your Progress

Watch Where You Are Going

To set a vision which is relatively distant and not achieve results immediately can become a bit frustrating and, worst of all, discouraging. Discouragement is to be avoided at all costs! If, however, you happen to find yourself experiencing it, remember that lasting success is achieved in small, manageable steps. Results may only trickle in gradually at first. But rather than dismiss them as insignificant, take time to record each one, however seemingly marginal.

Writing down the small results, in a place where you can refer to them regularly, clearly registers in your unconscious mind how you are on track towards not only your vision but also the fulfilment of your lifelong purpose. Keeping track will give you encouragement. Also, if despondency does creep up on you, you have a written record of your accomplishments to date to inspire you. *Superlife*, one of my earlier books, will also offer you many ideas to overcome discouragement.

Holding steadfastly to your purpose as you encounter the seeming rapids and apparent obstacles on the way to your destination will reward you with real inner riches.

> If one advances confidently in the direction of his dreams, and endeavours to live the life which he has imagined, he will meet with a success unexpected in common hours.
>
> *Henry David Thoreau*

Setting a Clear, Workable Intention

Immediate Objective

A journey of 1,000 miles starts with the first step.
Chinese proverb

Identify a workable objective which you would like to accomplish in the next month. The purpose of this exercise is to discover the ease with which you can attain it through careful anticipation and open planning. First and foremost, it is an exercise in learning how you can become successful with greater ease than you may have experienced up until now.

You will be:

1. Finding out what works for you, so you can do more.
2. Finding out what does not work for you, so you can do less.
3. Experimenting with new creative approaches, possibly unique to you, which prove successful for you.

You will find it helpful to commit your thoughts to paper so that you can refer to them and use them both to track progress and to keep on track. The following headings will guide your planning.

INTENTION

The statement of what you would like to accomplish (in alignment with your lifelong purpose if you have discovered that already).

SUPPORT

The friends who will best be able to give you encouragement when you need it. When you set an objective that is meaningful for you, it is likely you will be challenging a 'comfort zone' of former expectations, attitudes and behaviour. The support of loving friends can be very important as previous limitations try to assert themselves with discouragement, doubt and fear.

EXPERIENCE

Statements setting out how you would like to

experience **(I)** the process of accomplishing your objective. Make it the best possible experience you can imagine. Include soft images of ease and nurturing.

POSSIBLE ACTIONS

It is likely that the actions you need to take will evolve over the period of a month. Nevertheless, make a note of say three to five actions you *might* take, as far as you can tell right now. Aim for flexibility, with the possibility of unknown resources and insights to assist you when you may least expect it.

I would not go as far as to say 'expect' a miracle, because that might make you lazy. You could, however, anticipate a miracle as you move into action. Miracles start with your choice **(I)** to co-operate **(O)** at a high level with whatever comes your way as you keep your eyes set on your objective. 'Attitude' always and in all ways is the magic word that makes for miracles.

The following example illustrates this process with one objective.

INTENTION

To alleviate my addiction to stress and the pressures associated with my obsession with working as a primary reason to live.

SUPPORT

Susie –   my counsellor – set up some
          appointments for the month.
Frank – he's always good for a laugh.

Bob –   I can rely on his sweet nature to listen to
me.
Shirl –   she is so brave and gives me great
encouragement.
Jeff –   he is really good in helping me to see
around difficulties.
Teri –   her letters are an inspiration to me.
Ron –   that man is so wise, relaxed, humorous
and full of good ideas.

Yeah! What a *team*!

EXPERIENCE
I am building my inner strength daily with
conscious self-care.
I am receiving the most extraordinary support
from my wonderful friends.
I witness apparent 'miracles' of perfect timing and
'divine providence' stepping in when I least expect
them.
I increasingly enjoy my beautiful life.
I am increasing my love of life as a whole.
I am loving the music in my life, my harmony of
thought and action.
I am choosing happiness as my everyday reality.
I am tasting a new sweetness emerging in my daily
life, fresh like springtime.
I feel and am abundantly blessed through all of my
challenges.
My objective is fulfilled with outstanding ease and
grace.

POSSIBLE ACTIONS

- Let my team know the objective I am working with.
- Be clear about the time I will stop work each day, including not taking work home at the weekends.
- Research fun activities I will enjoy for the extra time I have available.
- Explore with my counsellor my motivation/needs for overworking and find ways I can fulfil those needs more effectively.
- Plan the treats and rewards I will give myself for whatever progress I achieve in the next month.

This is an outline that will work. You will only discover how once you work it. With practice, you will not need to follow it to the letter. In time you may well find your own creative adaptations as you practise it within different areas of your life.

At the end of the month, you can evaluate and make modifications based on the results you experience (I) and achieve (O). The main value in achieving outer results will be in the inner strengths you build throughout the process. These inner strengths can be transferred into your next spheres of activity. Also, *recognizing* and *appreciating* your inner strengths will assist you in developing a healthy esteem.

Effecting your Dream Daily
– from the Inside Out

Intuition, Attunement, Alignment, Spontaneity, Timing

Sometimes we may see ourselves as being alone, battling hard in an embattled world. This is far from the truth. As already mentioned, we are infinitely connected with all the resources we could ever imagine and more besides. What is more, we are not ultimately in control of all the events going on around us in the larger picture of life. All the time, decisions are being made, way beyond our direct sphere of influence, that are shaping our destiny.

You can, however, moment by moment choose to enhance your experience (I) of life, no matter what is going on around you. You can choose each day to adopt the attitude (I) and take the actions (O) that will amplify your healthy experience of life. When you have chosen an objective in line with your lifelong purpose of learning, you can literally 'tune in' to the most effective and productive actions that will support you in where you are going.

At the beginning of the day, you might like to envisage an expanded field of loving, see yourself stepping into it and ask the guiding light of your lifelong purpose:

'What would You have me do today?'

Throughout the day, you can remember to:

1. *Ask* inwardly for guidance.
2. *Listen* with awareness for your answers to come from any source (I) + (O).

3. Be open to *receive*.
4. Be willing to *act* **(O)**, or *not*, as directed **(I)**.

Using this approach, with practice, you can grow to trust yourself enough to respond spontaneously to the guidance you receive. What is more, you will discover how to work smarter rather than harder to produce the results you want, with much less negative stress, time and effort. You may also hear clearly when it is *not* appropriate to take a certain action. You will learn to trust the 'stop' signs when they show up and save yourself unnecessary pressure, stress and exertion.

At the end of the day, you can bring about a sense of completion and feeling of fulfilment by noting all your accomplishments, great and small in equal measure. They may not be great in quantity **(O)** but they should become increasingly sound in quality **(I)**. For example, you may find even a five-minute investment of time to relax and reflect pays great dividends. You may find this process in itself extremely rewarding and well worth the short time it takes.

Uncertainty: The Mother of Creation

Many of us feel more comfortable when we *feel* we are in control, even when truly we are not. As was mentioned earlier, the fear of losing control reinforces our limiting beliefs, attitudes and behaviour. Surrendering the control we *do not* have liberates us. But letting go of familiar attachments, even non-supportive ones, may leave an empty
feeling which is not at first comfortable. Typically, we are 'educated' to distract ourselves from this creative empti-ness with our addictions and dependencies, rather than

stay open to the gifts it has for us.

So, rather than reach out **(O)** for the cigarette, drink, television, chocolate, sex or whatever your usual source of comfort is, stop for a moment. Listen **(I)** for the real need underlying the discomfort. How can you creatively satisfy this need in a new way? How can you love yourself beyond your normal comfort zone?

> Love the one you are always with.
> That one is you.

Treat this approach as a loving experiment, not as a reason to punish yourself even further, if you find you do not succeed the first time.

At One with Yourself – At One with your World

INNER PEACE IN THE PROCESS OF OUTER ACHIEVEMENT

When we set ourselves objectives that are within our reach but not within our grasp, we establish a healthy inner 'tension' which is the energy required to accomplish our aim. It is the energy necessary to motivate us to get from point 'a' to point ' b'. Staying focused on our vision maintains the level of energy we need to ensure we are successful.

This motivational energy may feel like fear sometimes. But, as discussed before, fear might more accurately be identified as the energy of excitement. Rather than run from the fear, stay with it. Observe it in detachment. It may have information contained within it. As you sit back and watch it, you will receive the insight guiding you how positively to use that gift of energy.

Notice, both inwardly and outwardly, how you feel. Your feelings are valuable indicators that will assist you in making wise choices of thought and action. At first, this may seem easier said than done. In the midst of experiencing fear, you may feel as though you are almost in the 'inner microwave' of no escape. This is when friends and supporters are worth their weight in gold, as the saying goes.

When life seems to become too 'exciting' and you experience excessive fear, refer to the exercises in Chapter 3, Producing Inner Power, including those related to forgiving yourself *(see pages 104–6)*. Who you are is much greater than your fear. When you reconnect once again to the power of your loving, you reconnect with the profound inner peace that will facilitate your easy movement within the world around you. To misidentify yourself with a limitation, such as fear, is a mistake. So forgive it and move on.

Similarly, anger directed towards yourself or others is a misuse of the gift of energy provided for you to realize your **Dream**. Right beneath the anger is usually a residue of unhealed hurt. Below the hurt is the loving available to heal it. When you make the choice to love, you can heal the hurt and release the energy of anger for a constructive purpose. If you find yourself being self-critical because of your anger, forgive yourself.

When you cannot find an answer that you seek, relax. Uptightness blocks the energy, information and inspiration you need. Stop what you are doing. Take in a few deep breaths. Trust that you will be blessed with infinite opportunity for fulfilment. You will be.

Distinguishing Reality within the Dream

Clue: Look for the Loving

Realizing the **Dream** is a process of making tangible **(I) + (O)** that which you have envisioned inwardly. It will happen most easily when you connect with the warmth and joy of your gifts of loving. Too often, our experience of life has been a struggle to survive in a world of fear and conflict, lack and limitation. It does not have to be that way. The time can come when, through enough of us making the daily choice for loving, critical mass will make the world into an enjoyable 'schoolroom' it perhaps was always intended to be, a rich and nurturing environment for learning our lessons.

What if the end of the world as we now know it were not such a bad thing? The completion of an era of learning through pain of our self-judgements may make way for a new era in which we can learn through loving and forgiving, ourselves and others. It is entirely possible ... supposing it were part of the **Possible Dream** we all hold deeply in our hearts.

The **Possible Dream** is not a futile utopia, divorced from reality. It is not a rigid image of perfection against which you try to measure yourself and fail miserably. Your essential nature is already perfect and vibrantly alive. You can be the best you can become. Similarly, our world can be the best it can become – one in which we could thrive in peace and plenty. It will come through our choosing to love. That choice begins with you and I.

Chapter 5: Theme Exercises

Realizing the Dream

Realizing the **Dream** will come through your clarity of intention, productive action and personal enrichment through self-care. The theme exercises for this chapter will focus on inspiration and self-motivation.

Clarity is the result of being complete, handling your unfinished business, clearing out your dead wood. As you complete outstanding commitments, resolve misunderstandings in your relationships and take the time to love yourself you will have all the insight and energy you need to realize the **Dream**. Knowing clearly what you most want **(I)** will provide the direction with which to align yourself on a daily basis in all areas of your life.

1. *Feeling confused and uncertain? There is nothing wrong with that. As you let go of your patterns of control, you can expect to feel uncertain from time to time. Accept the feelings.*

   Complete and repeat the following statement to yourself a few times as you take in a few slow, deep breaths:

   I accept that I am feeling ...

Note: Be careful to say 'I am feeling' followed by a spontaneous response, which may change because feelings will change. Were you to say, for example, 'I am depressed' you would misidentify yourself as being 'depressed', when in fact that is only your feeling and deep down your inner being is joy.

When you lie to yourself, you deplete your energy.

2. *If there were one person in your life whom you have failed to*

forgive and love unconditionally, who would that be? You might not choose to move in with him or her now. That is not necessary. However, if you are unable to transcend the hurt you experienced, that hurt (I) may block you from realizing your **Dream***.*

You might like to make a point each day of repeating to yourself statements like the following until you are free:

I love and forgive ... for ...
I love and forgive myself for allowing myself to be hurt by ...
I forgive myself for judging myself as being unloving.
I forgive myself for judging ... as being less than loving.

As you repeat the statements, inwardly envisage yourself and the other person being surrounded by a clear white healing light.

3. *Experiencing enthusiasm failure? Exercise freedom with this exercise:*

   Bring to mind an occasion when you felt very enthusiastic, full of confidence and energy. How do you feel inside? Breathe into that feeling and expand it. Consciously smile (even if you do not feel like doing so). Your smile muscles will help to lift your spirits.
   Close your eyes for a moment to reflect: when you are really feeling your best, what is the word that describes you? Hear it being sung inside you; see it written in front of you in big gold letters; feel it rippling through every cell of your body. Savour to the full with all of your senses who you truly are when you are the very best you can become.

4. *Having difficulty overcoming inertia? You may be holding a vision which is so large as to feel overwhelming for you. What is the first very small step you can take that might*

take no more than two minutes? How will you reward yourself
for taking that one small step? Do not be tempted to do any more
until you have:

  a. Taken the action.
  b. Rewarded yourself for it.
Then
  a. Take the next very small action.
  b. Reward yourself for it.

Keep going with these very small steps until you are confidently
on your way.

For example:

  a. Make the phone call.
  b. Have a cup of tea.
  c. Mind-map how I would like the meeting to go.
  d. Go for a stroll.

5. *Love active (O); love passive (I) – strictly speaking you do*
   not need anyone else to experience yourself as the loving
   that you are.
   In this sense, one or more others whom you love and to
   whom you express your caring are a luxury and a special
   gift.
   Feeling abandoned? Reflect back over the past month and all
   the human contact you enjoyed, even casual contacts such
   as in the office, or in a shop, park or traffic. If you feel that
   one person has to fulfil your needs for loving contact, you
   may be short-changing yourself. Or you may have a lot of
   superficial contact but lack the depth or quality of love you
   could experience.
   Start with yourself (I). Breathing in slowly and deeply,

repeat to yourself with each in-breath:

I am love.

And with each out-breath:

I am loved.

When you next anticipate meeting anyone else, casually or other-wise, hold the intention in your heart to make a connection with the loving essence that they are behind the mask they may show the world. Find a baby and make eye contact. Find an old person and hold their hand as you send your loving through your touch. Tell your partner you love him or her in a way you have never done before.

Make that contact. The world is not short of people. You need never really be alone.

6. *Taking yourself too seriously? Suffering from a hardening of the 'oughteries'?*
   Think of the silliest thing you could possibly do, something which you would never dare *to do, especially if your friends were to find out.*
   Do it.
   Not that? Well, think of the next silliest thing. And the next until you have at least six. Do just one of them.
   For example:

1. *Wear a clown's nose for a day when it is not appropriate.*
2. *Hug the postman (maybe you already do).*
3. *Strike up a dance with the person in front of you in the line for the supermarket checkout.*
4. *Sing your favourite aria to a traffic warden.*

5. *Buy a bouquet of flowers and distribute them one by one to each person you pass on a busy street.*
6. *Hire a Superman outfit and wear it to work on a Monday.*

If you were to claim the freedom of your own spirit, what would it take? If you were to fully surrender to your joy, how would it be for you?

Wake up to the SuperYou you truly are: be the best you can become.

6

SuperYou ... Be the Best You Can Become

SuperYou and Success

Nothing Is What It Seems to Be ...
The old ways of experiencing certainty and form are gone.
All of the things that you used to gauge your certainty on
were based on past experience.
They don't hold up any more.
The new ways are about living the integrity and truth of
the moment.
And knowing that the next moment may hold something
that completely contradicts what was true in the previous
one.
This increases the necessity of finding a sense of certainty
in knowing that your inner wisdom knows what it is
doing.
Often while following your inner wisdom, things are not
quite what they seem to be.

It is a time to recognize that conflict cannot be resolved.
It can only be transcended by moving fully into a state of
knowing that Love is truly the most important thing.
More important than being right.
More important than your idealism.
More important than following the rules.

More important than feeding the illusion of your power over others.
Remember that Loving is the only true power in your life.

Anon

When we stop to think about it, each of us has a slightly different idea of what success is. Is it becoming a millionaire? Not all millionaires are happy people. If you want to be a millionaire, make sure you are first of all a happy person. Real success grows from the inside out (I)>(O).

Real success *is* possible. You are already fully equipped with all that you need to fully enjoy (I) a successful life (O). Any jolts that our changing world may be administering to you are the wake-up calls to tell you so! Many people are already realizing their **Dreams**. Why not you too?

The Possible Dream – An Ultimate Goal

What if the ultimate objective of your **Possible Dream** were much more than the accomplishment of all you want to be, do or have in your life? What if the ultimate objective were more to do with an inner certainty, a peaceful frame of mind (I) with which you can lead your life?

Peace has often been referred to as an absence of conflict but it is more. The 'peace that passes understanding' is a quality that defies description. It can nevertheless be attained and recognized (I). Securing a vision of peace is not a passive submission to the general drift of life as it flows all around you. It is a mindful, active and joyous commitment to the gift of your life.

The Possible Dream then might be a vision of a personal heaven on earth. It can come about, on earth itself, as more and more of us individually choose an objective of inner peace, an experience that goes beyond words and definitions and is simply known. That peace **(O)** might be the product of:

People
Enthusiastically
Applying
Creative
Excellence

Peace – A Higher, Creative Choice

Consider then that peace **(I)** is the goal, your active loving is the transport that will get you there and fear is what you are leaving behind. To enjoy the benefits of greater peace, keep your eyes focused on that direction **(I) + (O)**.

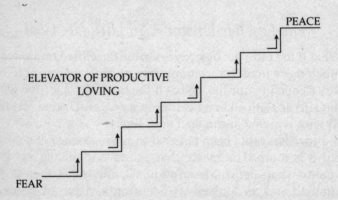

No matter what interim challenges you may encounter on the way to your **Possible Dream**, you can always choose a peaceful response **(I) + (O)**. The attitude of peace also makes sound economic sense. Fear is expensive, not just emotionally, but also economically. In conflict and fighting, the financial costs are astronomical and emotional suffering extreme.

Negative stress is often a factor in ill-health. Divorce becomes more costly when fear and anger dominate.

In peace there is plenty for all. A mind that is peaceful is creative, productive and open to new possibilities. Emotions that are peaceful, happy and relaxed are expansive, generous and full of good humour.

Innergetics © is the process that will enable you to attain the vibrant peace of your **Possible Dream**. The summary that follows illustrates the relationship between your inner world of thought, feeling and imagination **(I)** and the outer world of other people, events and circumstances **(O)**. *SuperYou*, together with *Superlife* and *Superlove*, offers you a peaceful form through which you can make the most of your life, from the inside out **(I) (O)**.

Innergetics©

A Summary

Innergetics©

is the art and science of positive focusing;
is the capacity within you to choose, maintain and sustain a positive attitude, no matter what challenges life may present.

Life challenges are the turning-points to enable you to bring out your best, to discover personal strengths and resources you never knew you had.

Innergetics© is about attaining:
personal freedom from fears, addictions and self-destructive habits, in order to be the best you can become;
happiness and fulfilment in your important relationships;
satisfaction, achievement and success in your occupation.

Innergetics© prepares you

*to become mentally and emotionally fit to move ahead in life:
to choose the best for yourself and have the confidence to
attain it.*

Innergetics© means:

*being ahead in your own 'game of life';
successfully meeting whatever life may present as an
opportunity;
pursuing a clear direction, with positive aims, objectives and life
purpose.*

Innergetics© is an expansive attitude of personal fulfilment
and success that enables you to
MAKE THE MOST OF YOUR LIFE.

INNERGETICS ©
MAKING THE MOST OF YOUR LIFE

SUPERYOU

Personal Values and Purpose
Attitudes and Self-Esteem
Care of Health and Well-Being
Leisure and Recreation

OVERCOME FEAR

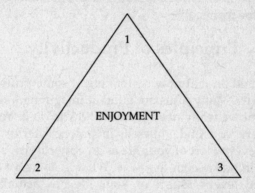

1

ENJOYMENT

2   3

SUPERLOVE   SUPERLIFE

Relationships/   Material/Career/
Sense of Belonging   Financial

OVERCOME   OVERCOME
SELF-DOUBT   DISCOURAGEMENT

Releasing your Loving

SuperYou is the powerful loving resource that sustains you. It can be recognized spiritually as that within you which is Divine, with which you are connected with life as a whole. When awakened, this loving essence has the capacity for envisioning an expanded set of circumstances, the **Possible Dream**, in the world. Through realizing the **Possible Dream**, you can be the best you can become. You can bring forward more of yourself, your loving, to overcome any internal obstacles that would stand in the way of your being the best you can become and you can come to know the true nature of yourself, which is loving and which is at one with all other life forms.

Principles of Productivity

Let's expand on that now by looking at some principles of productivity. Many of us are good at imagining a wonderful life, but we really need to know how to do it. You must start where you find yourself, in practical terms, totally *accepting* every facet of your life as an opportunity, even if it does not initially seem that way. What if, as we've already speculated, every aspect of your life has actually been brought into being by you yourself – for a very good purpose? Nothing that you have about you is, as it were, accidental. You may not happen to like it, but that is another matter! To like everything you have around you is a privileged position which can be attained as a component of realizing your **Possible Dream**.

So the *First Principle of Productivity* is:
In order to get what you want,
you have to *love* what you've got.

That means that there is no room for whingeing, moaning and groaning! Entertain a complaining frame of mind and you will attract to you more things about which you can complain. If you are a powerful creator, as many of us are, you will create an abundance of good reasons to feel dissatisfied. The energy of dissatisfaction is a drain on your precious life resources.

To put it rather more positively, every room in your consciousness must be filled only with that which you want to be creating more fully in your life.

The *Second Principle of Productivity* is:
If you are going to do it,
enJOY **it.**
Half-hearted action produces half-hearted results. Imagine yourself as a caretaker of horses whose twice daily task is – to put it bluntly – to shovel manure. You could have cause to resent the horses, their biological functions and the strain the shovel places on your back. Alternatively, you could put on a stereo headset with your favourite dance music and create your personal Disco in the Droppings. Shifting your attitude can make a great difference to the ease with which you can shift that other stuff.

The *Third Principle of Productivity* is:
Be selective.
Eliminate what you are not going to activate.
Choose wisely where you place your energy and 'deselect' those activities which do not serve you. It is not that you have a finite amount of energy available to you. The energy available is potentially infinite, but only when you are in alignment and step-by-step attunement with your vision.

You can probably intuitively, instantly bring to mind one area of involvement that is less than rewarding for you.

What is it? If you could give it up today, right now, how would you feel? We often entertain conflicting interests which drain our energy. Out of our heartless searching, we often take on a wide scattering of distractions which screen us from attaining those pursuits which are truly more meaningful, rewarding and, in the fullest sense of the word, productive.

When you experience fatigue or a sense of being overwhelmed, you might check to see whether you are attempting to fulfil agreements that are unnecessary for fulfilling your **Dream**.

The *Fourth Principle of Productivity* is:
**Be first effective
and second efficient.**
At any stage of taking action towards producing the results you want, choose first of all to 'do the right job' and secondly to 'do the job right'. It will save you time and energy. Or to put it another way, working smarter rather than harder will enable you to accomplish maximum results with the greatest economy of time and effort.

Knowing which action to take of the many options available to you comes down to listening carefully to your inner guidance. Sometimes this can come as a flash of inspiration and an irrational sense of 'knowing'. Taking the time to listen and to receive what is within you is an exercise in patience and wisdom which will pay infinite dividends.

The *Fifth Principle of Productivity* is:
**Love yourself.
Take care of yourself.**
The greatest demonstration of loving is self-forgiveness. Much like the horses mentioned earlier whose habitat requires regular sweeping up, so it seems to be in our

human nature that we drop negativity that needs clearing up. The negativity is in the nature of our misperceptions about a loving reality.

You need to love yourself enough to be willing to sweep up the negativity you have placed against yourself, other people or situations in the world outside. Were we to see the full picture of what is happening within and around us, we might be less hasty in making negative assumptions about people and events. The expansive view we can extend towards ourselves and others can only serve the fulfilment of our life purpose.

The benefit of loving yourself in this way is one of increasing your capacity for receiving, both inwardly and outwardly. If there were just one prescription you could have for a healthy, happy life it would be to take a dose of self-forgiveness at least once daily, if not twice. Self-forgiveness is an important ingredient of healthy living and an asset for realizing your **Possible Dream**.

The *Sixth Principle of Productivity* is:
Learn to say *yes*.
Increase your vitality.
The world seems to be well-loaded with prophets of doom, the forces of negativity, which will discourage you if you listen to them. You will find them abundantly rampant in certain newspapers and periodicals which distort for the sake of sensation and a quick (though very uneconomic) buck. The energy required to discern truth from apparent reality in such organs of negativity is an unnecessary expenditure on your part.

In learning to say *yes*, you will be affirming the truth for yourself as you know it and wish to become, 'know' being the operative word. For your greater health and productivity, stay well clear of that which could potentially pollute you and fill you with toxic waste.

Say *yes* to yourself and *yes* to your **Possible Dream**.

The *Seventh Principle of Productivity* is:
Focus on fun.
Be fun, have fun, do fun.
Fun is the pro-active, creative aspect of joy. Joy is the essence of who you are, which you can receive moment by moment, no matter what you happen to be doing. That resource is always there, as much as you choose to tune in to it.

Fun is the process of translating that joy into your everyday life. You begin by creating a fun environment within yourself and allow it to permeate throughout every aspect of your expression. The fun that you enhance inside yourself will be a part of the guiding light that will assist you to be productive in ways that are 'smarter rather than harder', economic in a real sense.

The *Eighth Principle of Productivity* is:
Own your natural abundance.
Cultivate abundance in your world.
You already have within you many seeds of creative wealth in the form of your talents, skills, assets and abilities. The word 'create' has the meaning to increase or grow. Not until you share your latent wealth with others do you fully receive the value of it. Your wealth might also be viewed as your 'well-th', well-being or self-worth.

You are abundantly endowed with resources which you may have yet to realize. Practically speaking, creative wealth translates into fulfilment in your self-expression, happiness in your personal relationships and material abundance, including money. As you give of yourself, you not only contribute to the wealth, and well-being of others, but you also grow to appreciate your inherent wealth or self-worth.

The expression 'opportunity only knocks once' is one of those false expectations that may have already led you to experience disappointments in your life so far. The reality is that when you stay dynamically open, opportunities just about knock you over.

The beginning of your personal experience of abundance may be that of fully receiving the opportunities to play with the many gifts with which you were born.

The *Ninth Principle of Productivity* is:
Just relax.
Agree with yourself that from now on you will nurture relaxation and a quiet mind. As in a fine English garden, there is a season for each of our experiences. The gentle hand of the gardener tends each plant with wisdom, cutting back as appropriate, sowing and harvesting in proper timing. The creative skill of the gardener is in choosing the relationship and positioning of one plant to another so that the play of light and shade, colour and texture come together in a joyful, exquisite harmony.

We each of us have the opportunity to own, honour and cultivate our gifts in the garden of our **Possible Dream**. The attunement with our personal rhythm and timing plays an important part in knowing when to act and when to relax.

The *Tenth Principle of Productivity* is:
Celebrate *you*.
Celebrate *now!*
Why not simply revel in the extraordinary richness of who you are, just the spirit of you, the essence of your loving? Celebrate now the gift of who you are, begin to receive the tremendous gift of your life, begin to live the miracle of all

that your loving essence has to bring into reality for you.

The stairway you are on goes up, infinitely. You can always choose to go down on yourself, but why would you do that? There's so much more fun to be moving on upwards. You can make it to the top of your own personal quest, your highest **Dreams**. Just keep moving up, don't you ever stop!

Become, *now*, the Superyou that you are
and open your heart to receive your Possible Dream.

Dear Reader

If, like me, you managed to grow up seeing your life as anything less than an extraordinary gift and the process of living as a miraculous revelation, I encourage you to explore the ideas and exercises in *SuperYou*.

In the process, I hope you will discover that your **Possible Dream** is truly within your reach and that you, as SuperYou, are more than fully equipped to bring it about.

When you have woken up to your true capacity for loving and valuing yourself, others and the world around you, you will find yourself at the beginning of the most magnificent adventure.

You are never alone. With others, you will be able to share the celebration that perhaps life was always intended to be.

Superlife, *Superlove* and *SuperYou* form the basis of the work that I do with individuals and groups of all ages and aspirations, assisting them to be clear about what they most want in life and to have the confidence to achieve it.

For details of the personal consultations, seminars and corporate trainings I offer based on the SuperYou Trilogy, please contact me c/o Thorsons.

Index

Of further interest. . .

Superlife

The seven steps that spell S.U.C.C.E.S.S.

Anne Naylor

Superlife is an astonishingly simple 7-step approach that will help you find out what it is that you really want out of life, clarify your thoughts and actions, build up confidence and inner power, and achieve success in everything you do.

- Set Personal Objectives
- Unlock your Attitude
- Clear Away Blocks
- Create Inner Strength
- Expect Success
- Simply Have Fun
- Start Now!

Superlife is a straightforward guide to personal accountability, choice and freedom. It is full of wit and wisdom, and a practical and inspiring companion for you on your path towards a fulfilling, successful new life.

Anne Naylor has developed a unique motivational and personal growth programme which she teaches both in the UK and the US. She has discovered through this work that everyone has an inbuilt 'success mechanism' which it *is* possible to activate!

Superlove

The guide to happiness in personal relationships

Anne Naylor

Superlove is an innovative and practical guide promising richer personal relationships, happiness, confidence and fun. Using exercises and examples, discover how changing your approach to love can open a gateway to expansion and opportunity, enriching all your relationships.

Anne Naylor has been involved in self-development work for many years. She specializes in helping people to get in touch with their own individual values, inner clarity and direction. She is the author of the bestselling *Superlife*.

'What makes Anne Naylor unique is her essentially practical approach. She gets you to start with self-acceptance and then keep going. You will end up smiling at yourself and others.'

Peter McWilliams, co-author of *You Can't Afford the Luxury of a Negative Thought*.

| SUPERLIFE | 0 7225 2600 8 | £5.99 |
| SUPERLOVE | 0 7225 2821 3 | £5.99 |

All these books are available from your local bookseller or can be ordered direct from the publishers.

To order direct just tick the titles you want and fill in the form below:

Name: _____

Address: _____

_____

_____

_____ Postcode: _____

Send to Thorsons Mail Order, Dept 3, HarperCollins*Publishers*, Westerhill Road, Bishopbriggs, Glasgow G64 2QT.
Please enclose a cheque or postal order or your authority to debit your Visa/Access account —

Credit card no: _____

Expiry date: _____

Signature: _____

— up to the value of the cover price plus:
UK & BFPO: Add £1.00 for the first book and 25p for each additional book ordered.
Overseas orders including Eire: Please add £2.95 service charge. Books will be sent by surface mail but quotes for airmail dispatches will be given on request.

24-HOUR TELEPHONE ORDERING SERVICE FOR ACCESS/VISA CARDHOLDERS — TEL: 0141 772 2281.